FIFTY
Christian Myths

JERALD MORRIS

ISBN 978-1-68197-798-0 (Paperback)
ISBN 978-1-68197-799-7 (Digital)

Christian Faith Publishing, Inc.
296 Chestnut Street
Meadville, PA 16335
www.christianfaithpublishing.com

Printed in the United States of America

INTRODUCTION

Reality and Myth: What It Is and What It Is Not

How many times have you asked yourself, "Do I really believe what I say to my friends, family, and strangers that relate to my understanding of Christian principles and beliefs? Do I really believe everything I have been taught from my teachers, Christian brothers, sisters, educators, and the many inputted sources that have contributed to my life? Do I accept what I believe, and do I osmotically adapt these beliefs and concepts to my existing Christian value system?" They are great questions and what a spot to be in! Should you take the challenge? Why not, you are already on the path to learn more. So go to the next step and win some more. Take the shot.

Fifty Christian Myths was written to address questions that are perceived by me to be very common in understanding basic Christianity, doctrine, and of course some theology.

The author is suggesting that you evaluate and examine your Christian etiquette, belief, and value system. Why not, who says you are right about what you believe in and propagate it?

We all have questions, and good questions bring good answers. Better questions bring better answers. Yes, congratulations, your finely tuned spiritual intuition has brought you to ask superior questions, yielding superior answers.

So what is this book about? Basically in a spiritual nutshell the size of our solar system, I hope to explain my position. I have produced a serious in-depth study of what I have compiled as my objective personal view of sharing notes, conversations, and observations between many born-again Christians, pastors, and lay leaders in Christendom.

After my conversion with Christ Jesus in 1977, I had many questions about Christ and salvation, and I wanted answers fast! I was surprised that I could not quickly get a grasp or a basic foundational understanding of Christianity unless I spent years going to Bible studies and church services.

So to alleviate that concern of my biblical deficiency, I started my own adventure and wrote in a journal that allowed me to collect and organize the hundreds of conversations, observations, and note-taking that pertained to my quest for biblical truth. My quest was blessed by God, and shortly after I got saved in 1977, I landed in a Bible college six months later. Wow, what a miracle, I thought. Who knew that would happen to me at thirty-three years.

I wanted to get on the fast track, but that was flying a fighter jet with a private-pilot license from day 1. I knew about one thousandths of a percent of a commitment to Christ, and Bible college changed that real quickly. Of course, we all can't go to Bible college, but we sure can get the basics quickly through diligent study and go from there.

My twenty-plus-year search has netted me amazing results that fortifies my foundational beliefs that Christianity is not complicated. Only it has a lot of parts that need to be assembled and get the full chronological picture.

I understood many Christians claim to know the truth of the scripture but are not sure they believe it. What I came away with is that many Christians have their own personal views with a varying rainbow of spiritual concepts. Some folks had a basic grasp that Jesus is the Son of God, and the Trinity is three spiritual persons named the Father, the Son, and the Holy Spirit. Many others simply did not get it.

Not one person in my research shared with me or understood the offices of God. Those offices are the Father is the author, the Son is the executor, and the Holy Spirit is the energizer. The three are always acting as one, and each person of the godhead does nothing out of context as to surprise each other. God moves in creation as a Triune God.

The majority of people I spoke with agreed with me that God works in mysterious ways, and that was good enough for them. My personal position is that our human condition, living in this physical world, is subject to the physical laws of creation, and we are energized by the spiritual laws of grace. That says to me, live and learn about yourself and the creation.

I believe these flowing spiritual nodes of thought identify the truth in pathways that underline our foundational personal belief system. My position is our Christian belief system is the anchor that is a composite of an interwoven, flexible fabric of secular and sacred thoughts to solidify our Christian total value system.

Our human experience as it relates to spirituality refers to the internal forces that motivate us toward goodness and the respect of the divine being that created humankind. If you are familiar with the term whistle-blower, it defines someone who speaks about injustices to a person or group of persons. Well, I am blowing the whistle in the last days, and I think it is time for it!

My exposé *Fifty Christian Myths* will educate you on the biggest competition in the world, the competition for your mind! God wants to save your soul from sin. Satan's game is to distort God's word, the world, and the minds of the saved and the lost.

The secular system of this world wants to use you and throw you away after it has gained what it wants and desires. The Christian community wants to educate you and bring you into the flock of the redeemed for Christian training and living in prosperity.

The whistle in this book sounds loud in its message that not all Christians are on the same spiritual wavelength. Personal and unbalanced views of life and the misuse of the scripture have crept into the Christian doctrine and way of life. This combination in many individuals' cases and in many Christian communities have corrupted sound Christian principles.

Spiritual competition is the fundamental superstructure that defines mind control. The world is full of control freaks. The Christian community is not exempt from these spiritual freaks that can attack your sound biblical values. We are saved from our sins by the power of the Holy Spirit working through Christ Jesus our Lord and Savior from God the Father.

After salvation, your mind is now super tuned to the spiritual forces that relate to good and evil. These spiritual forces are in a battle fighting in the spiritual competition to get maximum control of not just humans, but places and things.

Be aware that you are now on that frequency to know that good and evil are real and for you to seek God's grace continually. The spiritual universe is now open to you and staying on the straight and narrow road of spiritual understanding will keep you from falling into the pits of unbelief and unfaithfulness.

He and she are used in the contexts where it is applicable. My use of the word *man* or *man's* is in context as it would equate with humans. Be aware that there is no political correctness in the scripture, only the truth. Okay, let's go. It's time for a spiritual tune up.

The Propagating of Myths within the Christian Community

I believe Christianity in America is eclectic and divided. Attitudes and beliefs cross many cultural boundaries and lifestyles. This eclecticism and division range from sound biblical principles to fanatic believe-ism of what I see as reality and myth. For about two thousand years, believers have accepted the scriptures as the mainstay for spiritual guidance.

My observations are composed of a surface examination of Christian history, conversations, writings, and research. This work or quest has revealed to me that many Christians interject their own ideas into existing sound doctrines, which can distill the foundational truth. As time moves forward, many of these distorted views have crept into Christian doctrine as a regular practice. When distortion interferes with truth, it can become a tradition or a twisted view of the truth and produce reality or myth.

The root of a thought that can be traced to its origin and when documented produces a sound foundation. You can test it and draw conclusions. Speculation is spiritualization and that produces guesses. If you cannot trace the origin and verify the source, you are left with assumptions. From my experience, I have discovered that it takes time and grace to change the minds of people with distorted views who have not done their research to verify what they believe.

The main reason why distorted views hang on for so long is that they create negative habit-forming anchors of belief without proof of cause and action. My observations are that many Christian leaders by error intermix what they personally believe and compromise the scripture's literal word. It is atrocious and appalling, but not new to us who know that the spiritualization of the scriptures happens in many churches and Christian organizations.

'Example: take a close look at the **Nativity** scene. Most displays on Church property and people's houses show the Shepherds and wise men bringing gifts to the Baby Jesus in the Manger. Well, we know that is not true because the Bible says the Shepherds came from the fields to see the Baby Jesus in the Manger. The Shepherds were notified by a Personal Visit from God's Angels who guided them to the Savior.

When King Herod (that would the Herod the Great raised as a Jew and also a murderer) was asked by the wise men about the birth place of The King of Jews Herod was troubled. Herod did not readily have this information to give to the wise men. So as the Scriptures tell us, Herod gathered the Chief Priests and scribes of the people (local Jews) to ascertain the exact time and place of Jesus Birth. He finds out that it was prophesied that the King of The Jews would be born in Bethlehem. It was later Herod secretly contacts The Magi and tells them to go to Bethlehem and find the child so he may worship him. Herod wanted to know when the Star appeared to the wise men. It is obvious to me that Herod was running the numbers. How old was the Christ? Time and Place for this event would give that information to Him. We know he did not get it because the wise men did not return to Herod. So Herod (we don't know when) ordered all male children two years of age and under killed.

Remember the Magi saw the Star in the east and this was the same Star that led them to Bethlehem at a later date to find The Messiah. I deducted from the Scriptures that the Magi were in Jerusalem after the Birth of Jesus because Herod asked them about the birthplace of Jesus and The scriptures state Jesus was already born. As far as communications were concerned the Magi did not have smartphones, internet or walkie talkies and had to travel on foot. Notice the text in **Matthew 2.**

I quote, "After Jesus was born in Bethlehem in Judea, during the time of King Herod, Magi from the east came to Jerusalem ² and asked, "Where is the one who has been born king of the Jews? We saw his star when it rose and have come to worship him." As the God spells it out in The Scriptures, it was later that the Magi followed the same Star appointed by God to guide the Wise men to the place where Jesus was and it was not to the manger. The Shepherds in the fields nearby already saw the baby Jesus, the Magi were nowhere to found.

The question is; how can the nativity scene show the shepherds and the Magi at the same place and time worshipping the Christ? The Scriptures state it was the shepherds who worshipped Jesus in The manger, not the Magi. The Truth is even though the Magi who were from Persia and priests of Zarathustra religion 1050 Miles or 1700 Kilometers away from Jerusalem, they could not have been at the manger before the Shepherds.

If you do the Calculations the Magi had to be in Jerusalem or on their way before talking to Herod about where the Messiah was to be born. The Magi were being consulted by Herod as to the exact time the Star appeared. How much time passed between the Shepherds and the Magi and Herod, who knows? It is clear to me The Shepherds and The Magi were not in Bethlehem at the same time and place at the Birth of Jesus. If you map Jerusalem and Bethlehem which is about 7 miles apart, that means the Magi had to walk or ride their camels at least 7 miles from Jerusalem where King Herod

Reigned to Bethlehem. It was later that the Magi found the child Jesus in a House, not a manger.'

What's the point? Read, my friend, and read well.

Is there a base source in which we as Christians should draw from to interpret the scripture? Yes, there is. Look at 2 Timothy 3:16–17, "All Scripture is inspired by God and profitable for teaching, for reproof, for correction. For training in righteousness; that the man of God may be adequate, equipped for every good work."

There is no question that God's word is adequate for our learning, and we should always remember it, apply it, and love it. We in no way have the right to tell any person that our private interpretation is the only way a Christian should operate (see 2 Peter 1:20–21).

All points considered, our Christian leadership is on the right track. We can rely in our faithful brothers and sisters who are serving in the Lord's work. The people that need to be addressed are those who are not following God's teaching and are influenced by the world system and making value judgments, rules, and regulations that are contrary to sound Bible doctrine

Since my conversion with Christ Jesus in 1977, I the author have compiled an amazing number of phrases, conversations, doctrinal questions, answers, and quotes spoken and repeated by Christians that demonstrated to me what I consider a composite real-time eclectic compilation of spiritual views. This includes traveling in America, Russia, and Estonia.

During those extensive travels, I engaged in various conversations with many different people about God and how God works and interacts in our personal lives. I took exact notes and compiled them into a comprehensive notebook of what I considered worthy data from Christians. I researched them to the exact point of getting to the biblical truth of each quote, question, and answer. What I came away with is the clear understanding that most of those thoughts, quotes, and views are biased and depicted what many Christians believe as sound thinking in their belief and practice of Christian principles.

I have combined my research and titled this exposé, Fifty Christian Myths. Your guide to assist you is the scriptures (the Holy Bible) that accompany each quote and for you to maintain the scriptures as your foundational guide to *support or refute* the context of each supposed reality or myth. It is up to you to utilize use your critical judgment in order to find the truth.

All quotes, statements, or positions I comment on may seem absurd, obnoxious, outrageous, and contrary to what you believe or understand about biblical principles. Use your own judgment. I have no desire to influence your base of interpretation. I think it is time we get the errors out of what is thought of as biblical truth for daily living and use your spiritual common sense to drill down to the truth.

We need to let the scriptures speak with the power of the Holy Spirit without mixing human worldviews. This will prevent us from creating a composite half-truth based on our personal view of human interpretation and understanding to live the Christian life. God bless you for reading this exposé, and I pray that the Lord Jesus Christ will become more defined in your walk with Him to seek His truth.

As you make your journey through this exposé, I suggest you use the following twelve guides for scripture interpretation. This frame was adopted many years ago by serious Bible scholars and modified by me the author.

12 Guides for Scripture Interpretation

1. Is this a local passage?
2. Is the passage universal?
3. Is this passage timeless?
4. Is this passage a biblical absolute?
5. What is the context of this passage?
6. Who wrote this scripture passage?
7. Who is the target audience?
8. What version of scripture am I using?
9. Did I do enough research work to justify my position for my interpretation?
10. Does the language and the culture that I am addressing utilize language concepts and beliefs that are different than my own language and culture?

11. Am I willing to deal with the reality of the changing times and apply the scriptures as a spiritual guide and not legislate humanistic laws that sound like the scripture?
12. How can I apply these scripture passages today in my time and place?

Remember God has given us life to enjoy and live to the fullest in His will (see Genesis 1:28; Ecclesiastes 3, 9).

PERSONAL PRINCIPLES

Myth 1: Drinking Wine Is a Sin (see Romans 14:16–23; John 2:1–11; Ecclesiastes 3:1–22, 1 Corinthians 6:12; Colossians 2; 1 Corinthians 10:23–33; Matthew 9:17)

This old myth has worn out the welcome mat by pastors, lay leaders, and scripturally naive Christians. The drinking of wine is clearly explained in the scripture. The explicit correlation of passages on wine tells us that the drinking of wine is a matter of choice. The net result of the interpretation of the scriptures on the drinking of wine is that it is a choice to drink wine and not to drink it in excess. There are two general Greek words for wine in scripture, *oinos* and *gleukos*. The word oinos is used in conjunction with the fermentation process of wine. The Greek word gleukos is another term for wine, which also uses the fermentation process, in which both words have the meaning of intoxicating properties.

The scripture warns us that the drinking of wine in excess can cause us to have a distorted view of God and man. The scripture also teaches us that we have a free choice to drink wine. If it causes you problems or causes your brother to stumble, then you should exercise judgment in its use for yourself. The misinterpretation that originates from drinking wine in the Christian community is a distortion of what the scriptures actually teach on the subject. Somehow the guilt trip forced on Christians that drinking wine takes away our spiritual righteousness. You know that position is not true. We don't need to shun the gospel because we think it needs to take a holiday.

Many Christians have a terrible guilt feeling about the consumption of wine. Look, friend, when you read the scriptures, it is clear they speak about the individual use of wine. If you can't handle it, leave it alone. Please don't legislate morality codes for others because you don't approve of or partake in some wine. What right do you have to judge others? If drinking wine was a sin, how come Jesus Christ the Creator of the universe changed the water into wine at the marriage feast at Cana?

By the way, the Hebrew word for wine is *sikera,* a strong drink. The Greek word for wine in John 2:1–11 is oinos, it is the correct Greek word that describes the fermentation process that causes intoxication in wine. Think about it! The author is not advocating the drinking of wine! It is a cheap trick to tell your Christian brethren that drinking wine is a sin when in fact according to the scriptures, it is not a sin! If you choose to drink wine, that is your business, and it should be between you and the Lord.

Please allow others to make that choice for themselves. Please don't legislate morality for others, which are based on your narrow-minded, negative, counter-productive interpretations. In America, we are concerned with giving wine to minors, civil laws versus the scripture. Legalism is alive, but that does not dictate the facts of the scripture. Let the Bible speak for what it is, the truth.

Myth 2: Attending the movies is a sin (see Romans 14:16–23; Colossians 2).

Certain people in the Christian community attach this stigma to many movies that are controlled by the Motion Picture Association of America's (censorship) rating system. Many Christian leaders consider movies controlled by this group and TV Parental Guidelines as nothing but short of trash in content. These groups are not considering your Christian perspective or scriptural beliefs. The movie industry is about making money. Now that you know that, we need to evaluate our motives for any movie that we watch.

Basically, the scriptures speak out on the pollution of the mind from many sources, and evil movies are definitely a source. Evil movies are not to be enjoyed by the Christians for entertainment purposes. However, if you are going to a supposed trash movie for the purpose of evaluating the morals and corrupt messages that are being transmitted to you and your children, then do it.

You need to know what the enemy is perpetrating around you. How are you going to know what is happening in the world of arts and entertainment if you lock your mind away in a vault of denial? Remember movies are a reflection of the mind of man and a reflection of our times. The Christian must use his judgment and evaluation in non-Christian movies. Use your spiritual common sense.

Myth 3: Dancing is a sin (see Romans 14:16–23; Ecclesiastes 3:1–22).

Check the scriptures, Christian friends. The Hebrews enjoyed dancing, and Jesus certainly did not condemn it. *No dancing* is someone's immature idea of cutting out enjoyment for the Christians. What is the real motive that supports Christian's legalism on this issue? It can't be anything else but selfish want of control of your mind by selfish Christians with negative, counter-productive mindsets and attitudes.

What is so wrong with enjoying this natural free form of expression? I say it does nothing wrong! The early Christians and Hebrews were dancing and were quoted in many parts in the scripture. These negative Christian programmers want you to believe that it wires your emotions and gets the juices flowing that lead to sexual perversion, and before you know it, an intimate relationship develops and is out of control. Awe gee, poor baby, can't handle being an adult. Give me a break.

Dancing is healthy and one of the few pleasures that is free. If you are in this legalistic camp of propagating your immature ideas on adults, you're in for a long ride to nowhere. Who do you think you are to legislate your narrow-minded ideas about sex to adults?

If you support dancing is a sin, do you really expect adults to agree with you without question? Free will is operating whether you know it or not. Adults are supposed to make their own free choice concerning what is right or wrong. If you have a problem with dancing, then keep it to yourself. Who really cares what you think about something that is none of your business. What would your suggestion be to Christians whose profession is in the performing arts? If you told them dancing is a sin, how would they react? When was the last time you went to a ballet? What about Christians who choose theater as a profession? This Myth is nothing short of being silly. If you think dancing is a sin, you need your head examined, partner.

Myth 4: I can't eat meat (see Romans 14:16–23; John 21:4–5).

Who said so? This is another myth tied to the ankles of Christians. We do not eat meat by free choice. Where do the scriptures command us not to eat meat? Only under certain circumstances such as meat strangled or sacrificed to idols should not be eaten. In fact, this passage pertains to the Hebrews who were under the law in the Old Testament. In 1 Corinthians 10, Paul discusses that eating meat sacrificed to idols is no problem for the Christian who can handle it with a clear conscience. When Paul warns us about the eating of meat sacrificed to idols, it actually deals with your personal knowledge of knowing the source of the meat. If you can avoid it, then do so. Don't let legalism take over your spiritual common sense.

Paul the apostle explains that if you and your brother know that the meat was sacrificed to an idol and you are the stronger of the two and you can handle it but your brother can't, then don't eat the meat for conscience's sake. Don't allow your brother to stumble because of your own free will.

The New Testament says if eating meat or drinking wine causes your brother to stumble, then don't partake of that which causes the offense. Otherwise, enjoy all the meat you can eat. There is a passage in the gospels that clearly demonstrate that eating meat is not a problem; this passage refers to Jesus when he asked his disciples, "Do you have any meat? Please don't go overboard on this issue. It is your free choice to say yes or no. Use your own judgment.

Myth 5: Long hair and a beard are sure signs that a person is dirty and belongs to a sublevel position, below normal humanity (see Romans 14:4).

This thinking has been directly passed down from the changing times of human interaction during the 1960s in America. That time was a turning point of individual rebellion toward the establishment. That rebellion was to capitalize on the individuality to extricate the self to accentuate the uniqueness of the personality. It was the tune of the day. The time of change and rebellion for Americans was associated with beards, long hair, music, sexuality, and clothes that classified and exemplified degenerates and misfits labeled by the establishment. This attitude is cruel and very immature and still exists today, pierced ears, nose, tattoos, etc. If a person wears a beard or long hair or has tattoos or whatever, it is none of your business. Beards and long hair have been around for a long time. Gee, maybe the usual suspects now wear thongs and hip huggers and have tattoos? If you look at many paintings of Jesus and his disciples, you see in those depictions that beards and long hair were common in the first century! Get over it. Think about it.

Myth 6: It is wrong to be angry (Mark 11:15–18).

Controlled anger is vital to your sound mind. It gives you an outlet from your inner tensions. It demonstrates to invaders to stay out of your private business to back off and wise up. If your anger causes you to sin, then you are not dealing with constructive anger. Take the example from Jesus when he chased the moneychangers out of the temple. Jesus displayed a righteous anger, and it got the message across that the House of the Lord is a House of Prayer.

Please don't fall into the trap that anger is not healthy. Many psychologists will agree that there are many trying times in a person's life, and constructive anger is a part of that network. Be smart and accept yourself, learn about yourself, and learn your emotions have many facets. Do not let the devil get a foothold. Clear the air and move on.

Myth 7: It is wrong to be wealthy and enjoy it (see Matthew 20:15; 1 Timothy 4:4–5).

Many Christians are wealthy and enjoy their lives to the fullest. The idea that Christians cannot be wealthy and enjoy themselves is a misinterpretation of the scripture. Some people who believe this idea have more than likely been seeded with someone else's narrow-minded idea that money and servanthood do not go together. This attitude and mindset of money and servanthood not going together is out of sync with reality. These prophets of doom who believe money and servanthood do not go hand and hand have missed the point of understanding God's blessings to the Christians.

Many Christians think it is a sin to have wealth. The thought is that somehow money and Christianity do not go together in harmony. The truth is the scriptures teach that wealth is a blessing from the Lord. Wealth is a gift from God just like all other provisions that God gives to His people. The scriptures clearly teach that it is right to be wealthy and increase that wealth manyfold. In any venture, you must have order, definiteness of purpose, and the desire to win. How else are you going to get ahead?

The scriptures, Old and New Testaments, clearly define that riches, wealth, and money must be controlled and managed with the proper spiritual attitude. It is the love of money and not the love of how to create it and manage it that will control you. You cannot serve God and mammon. Do not confuse principle and purpose with greed and selfishness. We Christians who are obedient servants are responsible to share that wealth and to be good stewards of it. Read the parable of the talents in the gospels and the first chapter of Colossians.

Myth 8: Getting into debt is a sin (see Matthew 18:24, 27–30).

This myth has been a stumbling block to Christians for centuries. Here is what the scriptures actually teach about getting into debt. (Pay close attention you theologians who think you have it right). Getting into debt is not a sin nor is it wrong. Yes, that's right, getting into debt is acceptable among Christians! How is this so? Aren't we supposed be poor and humble to please the Lord and make an impression on unbelievers that our God will richly bless us? Does this poor-me attitude illustrate that we are blessed and that by not getting into debt proves we are good servants and good stewards of our money? Baloney!

The truth about getting into debt is to understand the principle of getting into debt. In order to buy a car or a house, you must take out a loan if you don't have the cash. This is getting into debt. It is legal, it is scriptural, and it is related to our society. In America, we live in a society where money is used as a tool to buy and sell. If you borrow money with the intent of not paying it back or you borrow money for selfish reasons which are questionable, then you are more than likely getting into debt for the wrong reason, and that is a sin.

Getting into debt is not a sin. If you are borrowing money to pay off illegal debts and borrowing money just to spend it on unnecessary expenses, you are borrowing for the wrong principle. We need the power and flexibility of borrowing money in the United States because we need a vehicle in which to establish our credit and help us grow and function in a complex society that thrives or a credit/cash flow system. Wake up to the real truth, read, and apply the scriptures. The only real debt that we all owe is love to one another. That debt can never be paid off because it is not a debt; it is a commandment from Jesus our Lord. "Love one another as I have loved you."

Myth 9: In order to be a good steward of all my money, I must buy only approved material and services that are related to prayer, fasting, and good judgment. If I don't follow through with this ritual, then I will be condemned for personal use of my own money for my own satisfaction (see Luke 16:1–13).

This silly myth has really been blown out of proportion. This negative, narrow-minded, counter-productive attitude stems from the idea that all the money we earn or accumulate is God's money and that we do not have a personal right to it. Yes, it is true that everything we have, acquired, or earned belongs to God. But according to the scriptures, we have the right to partake in our own earnings. The farmer has a right to his first fruits. No matter what kind of work you do, you are entitled to your first fruits.

Clarification

This idea of not having a right to your earnings is just plain nonsense, inappropriate, and unfair. This negative mindset is counter-productive to what the scriptures teach on wealth and earning a living. Listen, Christian friend, everything you have belongs to God. However, if you want to spend part of your paycheck to buy a new dress, CB radio, television or home computer, iPod, cell phone, etc., then you go and do it. It's your money, you earned it, and you have the right to spend it as you please. Don't get strung out on a narrow-minded attitude of stewardship. God does not need your money for His sake. God uses our money to further the gospel when we cheerfully give it through tithes and offerings, and that conscience giving is called proper utilization.

When we are good stewards of our money and give back a portion to God, we are in compliance and obedience with the biblical principles that God has given to us. The reason you give a portion of your money back to God is to give Him thanks for all the provision

He gives you. God will use the money that you voluntarily invest in churches and Christian organizations to further the gospel.

God cautions us not to be unwise with our money. Don't spend money on foolish things. Jesus taught that we should put some in the bank and collect interest! Remember to give back to God a portion of what you earn, and you will have a clear conscience about your commitment on giving back to God a portion of your earnings. You will be a happy soul that is contributing to the growth of God's outreach program to reach the lost and share in the earthly and heavenly benefits.

Technology and Progressive Thinking

Myth 10: Inviting new technology to church such as photocopy equipment, electronic typewriters, business equipment video, television, computers, the Internet, and satellite technology, etc., is sinful, and this is the way of the world (see 1 Timothy 4:4–5).

This silly mentality has been in the church and Christian organizations for years. It grows from the idea that we Christians are not allowed to use sophisticated tools to help us reach those who are lost from Christ. The thought is based on tools like technology invented by the world are evil and therefore, we should not partake on them.

Listen, folks, we have a mandate given to us by our Lord Jesus Christ to preach and teach in His name. We are to fulfill that mandate by whatever tool is available to us. Any tool whether it be a hammer or computer can be used for either good or evil. The instrument is only a device that is guided by motive of the human mind. When we apply biblical principles to the use of our tools, we will obtain biblical results.

If we can use radio, television, computers, satellites, networking, the written word, and mass media, etc., let's do it in the name of Christ Jesus. We are preaching salvation to a lost world that needs the love of Jesus Christ, and we must perform this command as clearly and as fast as we can. The redemption and salvation clock is ready to move into the next phase of redemption in God's overall 'systematic Chronology' for humankind's salvation. We need to take advantage of every legitimate tool that is within our reach. One day, God will call us home, and this job will be finished. Let's use what God gives us and glorify His name.

Myth 11: Watching television, reading non-Christian literature, listening to non-Christian music, and telling jokes are sinful (see Galatians 5:1, 13; 1 Timothy 4:4–5).

Many Christians are besieged with negative thoughts that non-Christian activities are sinful and taboo for the Christian. Not only is this thinking wrong and cruel, it is outright stupid and very destructive to the personality and character of a person. Where in the world do some Christians get the idea that they have to decide for you what your tastes and desires are? Who are they to tell you what you are to do in your own home and your private life? What purpose could it serve? It should be obvious to you that you are to use discretion in what you read, watch, and listen to and how it affects your Christian value system.

There is a lot of nonsense in this world, and this business of cutting yourself from the secular world is counter-productive. We know that the world lives by rules that are in conflict with God's word. We know the world is lost in sin and headed for hell as fast as it can. But there are real, worthwhile non-Christian activities that are refreshing and quite enjoyable for the Christian. Not all non-Christian activities can be judged and thrown into the fires of being evil. If you know what is evil, stay away from it. Many non-Christians are producing respectful quality work, and it definitely benefits the Christian. Your job is to tell them about the love of Christ. Enjoy life, and you will be happier and more people will share that happiness with you.

Divorce and Remarriage

Myth 12: Christians don't get divorced (see Matthew 5:32,19:26).

Christians are getting divorced at alarming rates. The statistics on divorce and marriage in America is that one out of two marriages fail and wind up in divorce or separation. That is a real shame, folks, because Christians are caught up in these statistics. Yes, that's right. Christians are failing too. Anyone can fall in the snares of the devil, and a sound marriage can fall to pieces and be reduced to rubble. Why do people get divorced? There are many reasons and scenarios and all boil down to divorce. It is a fact of life that some Christians will get divorced. In some cases, it is actually the best route for some because many marriages are doomed for failure.

Why? Because the two people who decided to get married might have gotten married for the wrong reasons. Marriages can fail for any number of reasons. It is the constant wearing down of the marriage that produces continual conflicts that lead to divorce. Good marriages have failed because influences and pressures contributed by both partners feel forced to get out. If you can hold your marriage together, then try it. However, if your spouse is unreasonable and will not live according to biblical standards, then you, the clear-thinking partner, must make a decision to leave for your own survival.

Marriage is always preferred as a measure of solidarity to one another than the divorce in a relationship. You must use every available means to keep your marriage together; if it fails, then do what you have to do and get on with your life!

Myth 13: Christians who are divorced are to be considered second-class Christians (2 Corinthians 5:17; Matthew 19:26).

According to the scriptures, we are new creatures in Christ. So if you were divorced, an alcoholic, a prostitute, a loser of all sorts, or a plain vanilla sinner, God gives you a new standing with Him in Christ. Yes, all sins are forgiven, and you become a new person in Christ.

Two questions you might ask yourself: What if I get divorced as a Christian, and how does it affect my relationship with God? The solution is to reconcile yourself to God through Christ. Yes, that's all! Seek the Lord's forgiveness, and he will see you as righteous as any other believer in his flock. Don't be misled by Christians who want to tear you down because you failed somewhere in your life.

We all fail at some point or another, let them, who criticize you, walk in your shoes if they think they are so pious! Who wants to be branded a loser all their life? There must be some justice in this world, and there is only in our Lord and Savior Jesus Christ who makes all things clean that was unclean. Jesus Christ has the power to call into being from nothing, from what did not exist. Certainly, He can forgive your little sins! Let God take care of you, and you will be a happy soul. Don't let the misled Christian tear you down because you got burned in a sinful situation even if it is your own fault.

Many evangelical Christians are two-faced when it comes to accepting the problems of others. Just because they never experienced the trauma you lived through, it gives them no reason to justify and condemn you. Once you have reconciled your conscience to God, no one can take it from you. Not all evangelicals see divorce and remarriage in that narrow context, but based on the author's own experiences, it was some of the worst treatment he received came from so-called loving Christians. Life always goes forward. You go forward.

Myth 14: It is wrong to remarry if you are a divorced Christian (see Matthew 5:32, 22:23, 19:26; Romans 7; 1 Corinthians 7; 1 Timothy 5:14; 1 John 1:9).

This cheap lie has hurt many Christians who have been persuaded and tricked by pastors and well-meaning brethren who believe that you should not remarry if you have been divorced. Parallel with this concept is the far-fetched idea that if the other person is still alive, you cannot remarry. Alluding to the other person alive also includes the husband-of-one-wife theory. It's complete and utter nonsense.

When you get married, you are married for life. When you get divorced, the marriage is over and no pastor, church, or so-called religious individual is going to change it. We have a legal system that sanctions our marriage vows and honors those who choose to divorce, utilizing the same power and authority granted by God. So what is the real story? What is the real deal on marriage, divorce, and remarriage?

God does not want human beings entering in a flaky marriage. The truth is that you can remarry if you are a divorced Christian. That means in most cases, the other person is still alive. The scriptures are clear that God is transcendent of all life! You are not going to marry in heaven or be given marriage in heaven. If you are skeptical of remarriage while the other person is still alive, you simply have a narrow idea of human relationships. The exception to any Christian remarriage is that it should conform to biblical standards.

You cannot marry and divorce anyone for insignificant reasons otherwise you are living in sin. "Ultimately if you feel bound theologically that marrying another person is considered adultery by the Scriptures, your out is to ask God for forgiveness. According to the scriptures anyone who marries a divorced person is committing adultery. Theologically yes, but committing adultery does not mean you cannot re-marry." Keep in mind that if you have a clear conscience and have reconciled yourself to God, then remarriage is for you. Living in sin is wrong. Remarriage is preferred over sinful relationships. Check the scriptures, friend, and let God guide your heart. Don't let any outsider's opinion about marriage make you unhappy because they think they know what is good for you based on their narrow-minded interpretations of God's word. God gave you a brain, use it. Matthew 19:23–26 states, "Then Jesus said to his disciples, 'I tell you the truth, it is hard for a rich man to enter the kingdom of heaven. Again I tell you, it is easier for a camel to go through the eye of a needle than for a rich man to enter the kingdom of God.' When the disciples heard this, they were greatly astonished and asked, 'Who then can be saved?' Jesus looked at them and said, 'With man this is impossible, but with God all things are possible.'"

The passage in Romans 7 discuss that marrying another person while the other is still alive is adultery. Paul the apostle was speaking to the Hebrews who were under a special dispensational law that was given to the nation of Israel. It was to be used as an example to explain that God hates divorce. It clarified that divorce is a serious dissolution of a two-party relationship that is bound by God's laws of commitment. Dissolution of a marriage is a soul-wrenching torture. Marriage is not a toy or a causal relationship. The marriage of a man and women is a special bond of two lives seen by God as one relationship. When that spiritual bond is broken, disharmony and disruption control your emotions, your good sense, and your spiritual harmony.

God hates divorce because it disrupts the ideal position of what marriage represents when two people live together as man and woman. When that union is dissolved, it generates unhealthy attitudes for the parties involved. Americans live in a land that is permeated with secular law under a system of that proposes equal justice for all. We Christians are under God's law of grace, which provides for our salvation, justification, and redemption in life as a Christian.

The law of the Old Testament does not bind us as the Hebrews were in respect to marriage and divorce. We must respect God's grace, working through our human laws and keeping in our consciousness the transcendence of God's mercy and grace. We are under the covenant of grace in Christ. We are also bound by the laws that we make in God's name.

What about divorce and remarriage? God still hates divorce. If keeping the marriage is impossible, then divorce or separation is a preferred choice rather than living in a situation that is destructive to your mind and your good health. If you can keep the marriage together, good for you. However, if the marriage is destroying your life, you need to make a decision that is healthy for your own sake. Divorce may save your life as well as your partner's life. By the way, God forbids quasi marriages for convenience and gay/lesbian arrangements. God is transcendent on all human relations and laws, which means God does not bow down to human laws. But God allows man to make laws to govern. Remember, God is transcendent of all His creations. God has given us his laws in the scripture and provides divine guidance.

If you get divorced, don't flip out over any churches or Christians' narrow-minded, restricted view that will leave you in a state of frustration and anxiety. You have a right to life and a right to rebuild. Getting divorced and remarried is not going to change eternity one bit. Don't get conned by people with overzealous, narrow-minded interpretations. Concern yourself with the process of getting on with your life. Don't use your eternal security in Christ for casual convenient marriages and think you have a license to habitually sin without judgment. Don't play games with marriage.

For additional readings, check out *Divorce and Remarriage* by Stanley A. Ellisen. Also a good resource is "Divorce and Remarriage in the Bible," Samuele Bacchiocchi[1]

---

[1] (http://www.biblicalperspectives.com/endtimeissues/eti_53.pdf).

Myth 15: Adultery is the only acceptable reason for divorce (see 1 Corinthians 7; 1 Timothy 5:14; Matthew 19:26).

Some Christians believe that adultery is the only reason for a proper divorce. It's not true. They are very misinformed. Yes, Jesus did preach that God hates adultery and divorce. The reason God hates adultery is that it damages the spiritual oneness of a marriage. It creates heavy guilt in both partners and insults the glorious sanction of marriage. Adultery is such a disgrace that in the Old Testament, a person could have been stoned to death for it. But in the New Testament, we have the forgiveness in Christ and are not under the law of Moses and not ruled by a theocracy. We are under grace in Christ Jesus.

Is there any option open to Christians for divorce that equals adultery? No, however, there are other reasons that are permissible for divorce. Paul gives a dissertation on this issue in 1 Corinthians 7. Many theologians believe that physical abuse of a mate, desertion, and extreme mental cruelty are grounds for divorce. Desertion can cover a number of reasons for divorce. Yes, there are legitimate reasons for divorce other than adultery. They are not the best or ideal reasons but are permissible. Stay awake, you have to live with yourself.

What happens if you choose to stay with your adulterous partner? There is an answer for any sin in any marriage. Adulterous relationships and any sinful act can be healed by the power of the Holy Spirit. We live in a complex society that puts excessive pressure on you just to survive. Sometimes these pressures interfere with a person's sound thinking, and a marriage can blow up and be more of a burden that a benefit.

When that is the case, you must use your spiritual common sense that puts survival first. It is better to go through a divorce than live a broken and defeated life. The scriptures are clear on the issue of divorce. Adultery is the spiritual end of the marriage vow. My position is that any person who lies and cheats his way through a marriage and will not give the other person a fair commitment deserves to be dumped. We are not under the law of Moses. We are under the grace of Christ. The scriptures are clear that divorce is a hassle, but peace is preferred to envy, jealousy, strife, and murder.

In 2 Corinthians. 5:17, it is very clear. (So whoever is in Christ is a new creation; the old things have passed away, and behold new things have come).

I am not advocating sin for a Christian. But we have to draw the line between legalism and spiritual common sense. Marriage is not a toy but also no matter what your human desire is, it is to help Christians make it through the storms of life; we each must live with ourselves. I have researched this issue many times, and I came to a point that Jesus forgives sins. Period. If Jesus cannot forgive me as a Christian, then why do I need His preaching of saving grace? I am sure many Christians want to take those passages of divorce and make a legal case out of them. Forget it. *They are not laws*, just passages of great guidance to assist us in accepting the unity of man and woman in an adult relationship that involves sexual and spiritual marriage.

No man or woman has the right to cause a divorce between another man and woman for false reasons. We are married in the eyes of God, and humans are witnesses. Divorce is the same concept. Sin is sin no matter how it happens. However, forgiveness is the key to Jesus's arrival on Earth. There will be millions of saved sinners in heaven, and many of the millions will have been divorced and remarried. There are human relationships with human thoughts, and God's thoughts are above our thoughts. What you do here stays here. Our sin after salvation is personal, and our salvation and redemption are personal.

It is true God hates divorce because it breaks the ideal sanity of a God-ordained and blessed union of two people who have sexual intercourse and a loving relationship without fear of guilt and sin. The key to this issue is motive. If you were starving and did not eat for three days and then you wander into a field of apple trees that are not yours, what would be your decision? Would you eat a couple of apples to satisfy your physical need for food, or would you pray for manna from heaven and a helicopter to take you to the nearest restaurant and fill up using your charge card, well?

Idealism is great but reality rules your life. Jesus saves and Jesus forgives us all. If He can't or will not, we are no better than condemned souls to burn in outer darkness because our God, Jesus Christ, who has the keys to life and death does not know us like he says he does in His word? Do you think that Jesus became one of us and that He forgot we are humans and that His love covers over a multitude of sins? Get with it, Christian friend. Jesus saves and Jesus forgives, period.

Sin and Salvation

Myth 16: Once you have accepted Christ as your Savior, you will sin no more (see 1 John 1:9; Titus 2:11–14).

The apostle John is very clear that we will sin as Christians, and we must seek God's forgiveness. Titus says we should live as godly people eager to do what is good while we wait for the appearance of our God and Savior the Lord Jesus Christ. Some Christians believe that we only make mistakes, and we really do not commit sin. Their position posits that it is possible for born-again believers to lose salvation because of sin in the Christian life. John tells us that if we say we do not have sin, we are liars.

The Bible gives us a clear definition that as saved sinners, we will commit sin. Understanding sin in the Christians life is to believe the reality that we still have a fallen nature that is open to sin. Yes, we have salvation, and the finished work of Christ on the cross guarantees that we have forgiveness now and forever. But we are not perfect, and God allows us to grow and discover Him. Through the growing process, we will commit sin in one form or another. God's mercy is everlasting, and God knows we will sin as Christians.

John tells us that when we sin as Christians, we need to come to the throne of grace and ask forgiveness through Christ who will clear our conscience of our dead works. Jesus said forgive your brother seventy times seven. Believe the scriptures, folks. The Holy Spirit will forgive you much more than seventy times seven.

Myth 17: I must be resaved after I commit sin (see John 3:16, 10:27–28; Ephesians 4:30; 1 John 1:9; 2 Corinthians 5:17; Titus 2:11–15; Ephesians 1:11–14).

This kind of thinking belongs in the spiritual trashcan. There is absolutely no scripture that supports this claim. Jesus never taught it, and it is diametrically opposed to the doctrine of eternal security. When we accept Christ as our Savior, we are washed and cleansed by the Holy Spirit. We are sealed for the day of redemption (see Ephesians 4:30). The devil cannot snatch you from the Lord Jesus Christ. Whoever thought up this immature idea of losing salvation or being resaved has ignored the eternal security proclamation of the scriptures. What kind of gift do you think God gave us when He sent His only Son into this sinful world?

Listen, friend, it is very easy to understand that God has given us a fantastic and wonderful gift, the miracle of regeneration! God planned and delivered us from the bondage of sin through Jesus Christ. It makes spiritual sense that God has provided us with salvation and eternal life in Christ Jesus. No mortal man or woman has the spiritual power that can break the seal by an act of the human will. Yes, Christians will sin just like any other fallen creature on this planet. However, we have the eternal cleansing of our conscience from our dead works through the power of the Holy Spirit. When you commit sin, you need to reconcile your guilty conscience to God. You are always saved. Jesus said, "I know my sheep, and they know me, and I give eternal life to them, and they shall never perish, and no one will snatch them out of my hand." Relax, Christian, and enjoy your life.

Myth 18: After I accept Christ as my Savior, I will have sinless perfection (see 1 John 1:9; Galatians 5:13).

Read Titus 2:13–14. No one has sinless perfection. Some people believe that they must become perfect in order to live up to the expectations to live a holy and blameless life because the scriptures tell us to do so. Yes, we are to live as holy people because we are called out from the lost world that we live in. But living a holy and blameless life does not include actually achieving perfection. We can never be perfect in our fallen state. We try to do the best we can with what we have. Don't go overboard with it. You will only find frustration and terrible guilt by pursuing a life of sinless perfection that is totally unattainable by human standards. God will guide us and give us our strength each day.

If you could really strive for sinless perfection, how would you do it? It is an awesome experience to live with the indwelling of the Holy Spirit. Make friends with the Holy Spirit and the real self, which is expressed through your personality, and spirituality will develop in the light of God's word and empower you to live a happy and fulfilled life.

Theology or Bible

Myth 19: Jesus did not know that he was God until he was thirty years of age (see Matthew 3:11; John 1:1, 6:69, 6:47–48).

Many Christians have the idea that Jesus was a man who only walked in the power of the Holy Spirit and that He did not know who he really was until He started His ministry at age thirty. In another words, Mary the mother of Jesus is also the mother of God, and all Jesus had to do was to wait until age thirty to realize it. This idea is far-fetched and minimal at best and absolutely not true. It is cruel and a disgrace to even think of such a thing. When Jesus was in His mother's womb, He was holding the universe together. When Jesus came to Earth and took upon Himself human flesh, He brought with Him His full attributes of God.

The Son of God existed long before the person of Jesus came into being and walked this Earth. Jesus, the Son of God, is actually the Word, the logos. He is God. While on Earth, He was known as the incarnate Christ. The doctrine of the *hypostatic union* discusses the Godman. Jesus, while on Earth, was the Godman, fully God and fully human. Can we comprehend it? No! Can we accept it? Yes! Jesus clearly showed us the mercy, and the justice of God. He showed us the Father by demonstrating to us the wonders of a loving God.

Jesus is the only person to have two separate natures, divine and human. We only have one nature, which is human. We all have a thread of the divine spirit of God, but as compared to Jesus, we have human parents. Jesus had only one human parent, his mother Mary. Mary provided a body for the son of man. When we are filled with the Holy Spirit, our spirit and the Holy Spirit share the same space. The Holy Spirit in our lives is our guide. He is not a second nature to us. We can only imitate and be like Jesus and not be divine and human at the same time. We are dwelled in by the Holy Spirit, and He gives us our divinity. Jesus was truly a unique individual. He is the Godman.

Myth 20: The God of the Old Testament is not the same God of the New Testament (see Genesis 1:26; Exodus 3:14; Deuteronomy 6:4; John 1:1, 6:38, 8:58).

Better put on your reading glasses again, Christian friend. A clear example of God being the same God in both testaments is explained in detail in the New Testament passages where Jesus Christ makes reference to the I ams in John 8:58 in contrast to the Old Testaments I ams in Exodus 3:14.

Please don't let anyone trick you into believing that God has changed his form between the Testaments. In fact, if you check Hebrews 13:8, you will read that Jesus is the same yesterday, today, and forever. That means God is the same yesterday, today, and forever. When Christians discuss the differences of God's actions in the lives of men in the two testaments, we can refer to it as dispensationalism. Throughout the scriptures, God has revealed Himself and His plan for man through the ages by the implementation of different and independent or related dispensational systems to cause man to realize that man is a created creature subject to God's love, mercy, discipline, and judgment.

God reserves the right to keep man in a balance so man will not destroy himself. God gives us witness to Himself through general revelation and special revelation. General revelation consists of the visibly created things. Special revelation takes its form in the actions and indwelling of the Holy Spirit in the lives of men, the scriptures, miracles, and acts of God that are set in motion completely independent from human intervention.

Yes, God is the same in both testaments. Jesus our Lord, and God are the same God in the beginning and the same God after the resurrection. To help you fulfill your yearning to understand how God works in the life of man, look at the completeness of the scripture and accept that God has worked in many different ways and in different times to help man believe and accept that there is one God who is responsible for man's creation and care. Through the many systems (covenants) that God has implemented, He has revealed His kindness, justice, and mercy to man in a personal way.

Myth 21: The King James Version of the Bible is the most acceptable version of scripture approved by the church. In addition, it is to be used for daily living by Christians who believe that the King James Version is the authorized version of the scripture (see 2 Timothy 3:16–17; 2 Peter 1:21).

Many pastors and Christian followers have been preaching and teaching this false information for hundreds of years. Yes, that's right, people, hundreds of years. The truth is that no English version of the Bible is the authorized version. Originally, the first KJV was the great Bible commissioned in the reign of King Henry VIII in 1535. King James gave the translators instructions, intended to guarantee that the new version would conform to the ecclesiology and reflect the episcopal structure of the Church of England and its belief in an ordained clergy. It's a great idea for man to be so considerate! Well, over the years, Christians have distorted it that the King James Authorized Version as being the original authorized version accepted by the church as the formal translation.

Talk about stupidity and ignorance, the King James only autho-rized formal translation takes the cake, the pie, and the cookies. If you want to get dogmatic about the real authorized versions, we should be preaching and teaching from the Hebrew and Greek text. Now you would get the truth in the original languages. That is a heavy punch line, but with today's legalism, it makes you wonder why Christians are so dogmatic about something they know very lit-tle about. Step up to the plate, Christian friend, and do your home-work and get real about the scriptures' translation.

Hebrew, Aramaic, and Greek were the original languages of the scriptures, and since their original inspiration, they have been trans-lated into many languages and Dialects these translation into many languages or tongues allow others to hear and read the gospel in their mother language. The scripture's versions we read today are trans-lations of those original or copies of the Greek manuscripts. God's word is the same in power, authority, and truth. It makes sense to accept translations other than the King James to preach and teach the Word of God.

Be aware that legalism and corrupt ideas have crept into the church's view of acceptable translations. In the case of the King James Version, it was translated from the Byzantine manuscripts. I prefer the NASB for the reason of accurate translation. You may differ with me and stick to your King James Version until the rapture. God's message is the main point in any translation, and you need to get that straight.

God's word will never change in its inerrant message no matter what translation you use. There are errors in the scripture and that relates to textual adaptations and penned errors. The definition of the word corrupt in the context of Bible scholars means "a translation with errors." These errors are in the form of gender, usage of nouns, and syntax. It does not mean that the King James is corrupt in its message. It only means that the translators, by accident, penned in errors because their fallible human nature was at work just like ours. By the way, errors have been found in translations other than English.

If you look at the many versions of the King James today, you will find many translations and retranslation of that version. All turned to the idea of making it more readable and conformed to the changes of language. The New American Standard Version is one of the best translations available today. It was translated from the Alexandrian manuscripts. It is approved by hundreds of evangelical organizations and Bible colleges today. Remember to use your spiritual common sense when declaring that a particular translation of scripture is the best or the only one to use.

How would native people in a remote part of the world perceive your preaching if you were using the King James Version from 1611? What if the indigent people did not speak English? Think about it! The New Testament was penned in Greek! Why? Because God chose it to be so and as it turns out, Greek was the most common language of the people in the country where it was penned! You might want to read *The King James Debate: A Plea for Realism* by D. A. Carson. Most importantly, read 2 Timothy 3:16–17 and 2 Peter 1:21.

Myth 22: I get a new nature when I accept Christ (see Romans 7:14–25).

We only have one nature. We have a human nature. When we accept Christ as our Savior, we are converted from our lost, sinful, and broken spirit to a restored, renewed, and righteous spirit in the power of the Holy Spirit in Christ. Our fellowship and our position are then counted as righteous because we have the blood of the sacrificed Christ applied to our souls. Our nature changed in the sense that we have a right mind and a renewed spirit that has instant righteous communication with our Heavenly Father. We still have a human nature but in this body of human nature dwells the Holy Spirit, which has a divine nature. The Holy Spirit is a deposit guaranteeing our righteous state of being in Christ.

Now our inner being is renewed and strengthened in Christ. We are free to discover ourselves and learn of the wonders of our Creator in Christ through the power of the Holy Spirit. Yes, that's right, you skeptics. We have the right and privilege to discover ourselves. When you believe in yourself and trust that God wants you to believe in yourself, you can have a clear conscience about your own individuality.

You can believe that God created you as you are, and you have the absolute right to love yourself and discover that God wants you to enjoy what He has prepared for you. That means you will be a happy soul, thanking God for every breath He gives you. It is within this context that you need to agree that you have value, net worth, dignity, and the right to live and breathe in God's kingdom. It is then with a clear mind that we can be proud and thankful that in our choice to serve God, we can put on the mind of Christ and be the best in Christ Jesus. We can shine for Christ.

Myth 23: I get a new personality when I accept Christ as my Savior (see Colossians 3:1–2; Romans 8:15; John 3:1–8).

No one gets a new personality when they accept Christ. Your mind and your spirit are now changed from not knowing God's will to knowing God's will. When you put on the mind of Christ, your attitude about life will change in the direction of pleasing God. Yes, your personality is altered in the sense that you know God, and you want to do His will, which is to obey Him and love one another.

When we are born from our natural parents, our personalities are a combination of our parents' DNA and the human spirit/soul God gives us at birth. Yes, there are different personalities, but it is intertwined with our physical makeup and our spirit. These two entities working together form a personality. Our born-again position restores our fellowship with God, and we now can explore and learn of our personality within our individuality through spirituality.

Remember God gives you talents at birth, and He gives you spiritual gifts at the time you accept Christ. Life is a continual process of developing and utilizing the gifts and talents to aid us to grow and share with others. Our salvation in Christ ensures that we have sanctity, justification, redemption, eternal life, and eternal security. Live for God and He will bless your life. Use all you have to be the best in Christ Jesus.

Myth 24: Speaking in tongues are a sure sign that I am born again (see Romans 10:9–10; Acts 2:38; John 3:16).

This myth has been very hard to deal with, especially since more churches have taken the full gospel approach. God gives gifts to born-again Christians that vary in purpose according to His good pleasure. Tongues are one of those gifts that are given according to God's dispensational giving.

The word tongues means languages. When Christians are speaking in tongues, it means they are speaking in different languages. However, when a tongue is spoken, there is usually an interpreter standing by to translate. The receiver of the tongue could be the translator of the message or a coworker working with the translator who will give the translation. Tongues are usually associated with the different dispensational time periods that the scriptures allude to.

The scriptures clearly teach that tongues are a spiritual sign to unbelievers. In addition, when someone is speaking in tongues, there should be an interpreter to translate the message. Moreover, the scriptures indicate that the gift of tongues was very active during the growth of the church in the first century.

You must remember that the first-century church did not have a New Testament to preach and teach. The men and women who were ministering to the unbelievers had direct revelation from God and the knowledge imparted to them from the Holy Spirit and the maturity of experience that they built up among themselves. Keep in mind that the New Testament had not been written in full or brought together into one book. Also the New Testament was penned in Greek, and there were no Bible translations during the first few centuries of early Christianity until many years later.

Speaking in tongues is not a sure sign that you are born again. The proof of salvation is being born again by accepting Christ Jesus as your Savior by faith. The proof of that faith is your proclamation that Jesus Christ is the Son of God in the power of the Holy Spirit. You are to witness that He has saved you from your sins, and you have a personal relationship with Him. We live our faith through our good works. Those good works according to the book of James are examples of our commitment and expression of our inward confession that we have the spirit of Christ in our heart. As a believer, we are secure what the Word of God says as our faithful source for the proclamation of godly principles for daily living.

Our good works is a witness to unbelievers that the Holy Spirit indwells us and that we are happy to proclaim the name of Jesus Christ as our Savior and Lord. Tongues have nothing to do with the act of salvation as a requirement to be saved or born again. If anyone teaches you that we must speak in tongues as a proof of salvation, he or she is a liar, and they do not understand Romans 10:9, Romans 6:23, John 3:16, Acts 2:38, and Acts 26:16–18.

Think about this, if tongues were a sure sign of salvation, ask yourself these questions, did I speak in tongues when I got saved? What about the thief on the cross who said to Jesus, "Lord remember me when you come into your Kingdom" and the Lord Jesus said, "surely this day you will be with me in paradise," do you see any inflection of tongues in those statements, Christian friend? In Acts 2:38 the question was asked, "What must I do to be saved?" Peter's response was "believe on the Lord Jesus Christ and you will be saved and you will receive the Gift of the Holy Spirit." Notice that tongues were not mentioned as the aftereffect to prove salvation.

The nagging question that is bugging theologians and Christians today is the question: Has the gift of tongues ceased as a vehicle to witness to unbelievers? The answer is for you to perform a methodical hermeneutic study of the passages relating to validity and dispensational use and application of tongues. Some were for unbelievers, and some were for edification between God and a believer.

Today we know that the Word of God has been translated into many languages or tongues and that we have a complete copy of both testaments. Paul the apostle says that tongues will cease. There is no definite date, or there isn't any positive time in which tongues will cease. God has invoked a dispensational meting out of spiritual gifts in our new covenant in Christ. God exercises the right to invoke any gift and that includes the gift of tongues at His own choosing.

Yes, one day, tongues will cease altogether in God's good timing. But to say that tongues has ceased for all time at this juncture in the new covenant is taking the position of judging the scriptures on the declaration and application of their local or universal use. In today's conservative views, man has for the convenience of things kept a lid on this gift because humans have a difficult time understanding and accepting this powerful spiritual tool without prejudice. You are safe if you are not involved with something that is not of God. If you speak in tongues and it is of God, you will know it for sure.

Myth 25: All liars are going to hell (see Revelation 21:8; John 10:27–28; Titus 2:11; Ephesians 4:30).

This passage has many Christians fleeing from peace of mind. It is one of the most misinterpreted scripture passages in the New Testament! It also has been used as a fear tactic by pastors to put fear into the unwary Christians who do not know the truth about eternal security.

Yes, that's right, a serious misinterpretation of this passage has sent many pastors and Christian followers into panicked states of mind. The passage says that all liars, whoremongers, and murders will not enter the kingdom of God. Is this passage true that all liars and others are going to hell, or is it saying that certain types of liars are going to hell? The keys to understanding this passage involve some scriptural detective work. Here are the answers to help you understand this passage.

This passage is directed to unbelievers only!

1. The church has already been judged. Our judgment is at the Bema Seat for Christian works, not sin. The shed blood of Christ has already forgiven your sin. The chronology of the scripture is clear on time and events.
2. If you do a word study of this passage in Greek, you will find that the contextual words liar (pseuds) and the word (pas) all are in a specific context that is used for unbelievers only.

3. This judgment of all liars is taking place at the great white throne of judgment, in which Jesus Christ is judging all unbelievers from eternity and are being judged for their deeds whether good or bad.

4. The comparative passages that God will not go back on His promise in John 10:27–28 is a proof that God promises eternal life and eternal security to those who believe in Him. These passages are a definite guarantee that we have eternal life in Christ, and we do not come under the wrath and condemnation of God.

5. Your spiritual common sense will tell you that God put Jesus through the most embarrassing, intolerable, disgraceful, and disgusting torture test to prove to us that He loves us and wants to share His kingdom with those whom He has called and accepted His Son Jesus Christ as Savior.

Why would God have Christ suffer so much for us only for God to take it away because we sinned somewhere in our Christian walk, no way! Read John 10:27–28. Read Titus 2:13–14. Read Ephesians 1. God loves you and that you have eternal life and eternal security in Christ.

Myth 26: God has only one will for my life, and if I am not careful, I will miss it, or I can even get out of it (see 2 Thessalonians 1:18; 1 Thessalonians 4:4–8; James 4:13–17; Romans 1:17).

Finding God's will for your life has been interpreted by many Christians as finding God's perfect and acceptable will that pleases God, and you leave your desires out of it. In other words, sacrifice all you have to serve God. Sell your house, give away your possessions, expensive cars, or material goods, earn a small paycheck and give 10 percent to the church, and expect nothing from the world. This idea of finding God's will for your life with the above-mentioned expectations has left many Christians living in grief and unexpected frustration for nothing. The belief that God has a rigid plan without flexibility will increase their faithfulness. In another words, God's will for your life is perfect and acceptable. The author believes that God's will for your life comes in distinct phases. God has provided salvation for your souls.

1. You are to obey the commandments.
2. Love one another.
3. Let the Holy Spirit guide your heart and mind through the application of the scripture, divine guidance, Christian friends, experience, and prayer.
4. God has a secret and revealed will for all people in His kingdom.

God's will for our lives is expressed in many ways. We are to love God and serve Him. In our desire to serve God, He will bless us with His love, which is expressed in many forms and many ways. Some Christians believe that God has a personal will for their life and that will cannot be changed or altered by an act of the human free will. That is not true. God does have a will for our lives. One aspect of that will is to serve Him in the ways we are taught by the scripture and guidance from the Holy Spirit. Salvation of our souls is another act of God's will for our lives.

Does God have an ideal will for our lives? Yes, he does, but you are not going to find out everything in one reading of the scripture. Finding God's will for our lives is a steady, on-going process. We are not locked in a box in which we have no freedom of thought. God has planned many things for us in His will, but you must allow for the secret things and the revealed things to be worked out one day at a time.

We have a free will that interacts with God's will, enabling us to operate within a system that is designed to let us serve our Creator. Please don't burden yourself with trying to find out all the exact details of God's will for your life. Only God knows the future. Obey the commandments, practice the principles of the scripture, pray without ceasing, and listen to illumination of the Holy Spirit when he prompts your mind. All these things are in the will of God.

Some people believe you can get out from the will of God. Many Christians have been heartbroken because they thought that sin in their lives broke their relationship with Christ.

Listen, Christian friend, God has clearly demonstrated in John 10:27–28 and Ephesians 4:30 that Christians are fully insured against any attempt of getting out of the will of God or losing salvation. In addition, we are insured in confidence that confessing sin to clear the conscience is a direct act of God. Don't listen to those jokers who teach contrary to the scripture. God does have plans that are in line with your life. You cannot get out of the will of God. You can goof things up with your stubborn free will to do your own thing your own way. Salvation is the will of God, and you cannot get out it. Hopefully, you will get that point. Let God guide your steps in this life, and you will do well in His kingdom.

Myth 27: God will cause someone to send a letter to my mailbox, telling me whom I will marry, the kind of job I should have, and how I am to spend my money as a wise steward (see Psalms 37:4; Ephesians 5:14–21; Philippians 12:2; Matthew 7:7–8).

This Christian myth says that God will in some personal way tap them on the shoulder and explain in great detail what their next decision is in life. When a person accepts Christ as his/her Savior, he/she is now placed into the body of Christ by the Holy Spirit. From that point on, a great plan gets revealed one day at a time. The observation is that many Christians feel that after accepting Christ, they are in tune with divine guidance that will make all their decisions for them, and all they have to do is wait for it. This kind of thinking is just plain fatalistic. Yes, God does have a plan, and He does lead you through the paths of righteousness. However, you have to put a genuine effort into your Christian thinking. You have to work with God so His will is perfected in you.

God is not going to make all your decisions for you. You have a free will that is in tune with God's universal spirit. Have you read the passage in James that outlines that we must be doers and not just hearers of the word? Have you not read that faith without works is dead? We are to live our Christianity. We are to be partakers of the things in this world. We are to enjoy the fruits of our labor. We are to serve God with a heart of gladness and reach for the stars.

Stop cutting yourself off because you think you deserve less because you are a Christian. It is not wrong to get involved with the world, it is wrong to love the world and be like it. Use your talents and gifts to make a better world. Use what you have to better yourself. God gives gifts and talents that are unique by individual use. Read Genesis 1; you will see that we are created in the image of God. We have a right to be here, and we have a right to life. Go for it.

Social or Personal Issues

Myth 28: Christians should not get involved with birth control, high-tech methods of fertilization, and adopting children from other races (see Colossians 3; Titus 3).

Christians must deal with diversity of new hurdles. Many Christian leaders are perplexed on how to deal with these new scenarios. Face the facts that we live in a complicated society. A complicated society has complicated lives. The Christian is a light unto this dark world. He or she is to announce and proclaim that Jesus Christ is the Son of God, and He fills our life with gladness the world system cannot provide. The Bible gives us our guidelines, and we are to utilize them in our daily lives.

God has given man a free will. He is created in the image of God with the ability to create and invent tools and material goods that are a necessary part of his existence. God has also given man the ability to create and fabricate tools and methods to solve problems. Within this structure, man has found a way to abuse the system. Man has fallen into the age-old trap of abusing the talents and gifts he has for profit at the expense of others. Examples like pride of personal gain that sacrifices the good standing and character of a person, stealing, cheating, lying, and capricious experiments destroy and maim people lives.

Explanation

In sensitive areas like test-tube babies and new methods of fertilization, it is biblically permissible to have children through this method. I believe the sperm and egg should be from a married couple seeking children' You may believe otherwise and it may be possible, feasible, and spiritual. Seek God's guidance don't guess at it. I believe the sperm and egg should be from a married couple living together as husband and wife. Also sensible birth control methods are preferred to the extreme position of bringing children into this world that will not have a chance to make it.

Birth control is a viable option for many couples that choose to limit a family based on income levels and plans and goals of the parents. Some people only want or can afford one or two children, and after they are raised, the parents want to get on with other plans and activities for their future. If you think birth control is wrong, then why don't you look at the natural birth control methods of the male and the female? Birth control is not wrong or sinful. The method that you use should be a sensible method that does not harm the body.

Considerations

A man produces billions of sperm that will never reach maturity or reach an egg in the female's body to cause fertilization. Many sperm are lost to natural emissions and natural selection when deposited in the female. Only one sperm out of millions reaches the egg if the egg is present in the female.

1. Women have hundreds of eggs that will never be fertilized because the sperm will not reach them. A woman loses one egg per month.
2. Natural abortion takes place in some women because their bodies reject embryos.

Reaction

Stop worrying yourself sick over trivial matters. Don't you think God knows what goes on between a man and woman's sexual life cycle? Please give yourself a break and enjoy your sex life.

Summary

In our perception of what is acceptable to God, we need to know what our boundaries are and what is not acceptable by God. What is not acceptable by God's standards can be interpreted from the scripture, the leading by the Holy Spirit and our spiritual common sense. Examples of non-acceptable matters for the Christian are abortion for profit; euthanasia; genocide; sex determination with the intent of killing unwanted sexes; ghastly experimentation and extermination of human fetuses; the starvation of babies that are born with birth defects; experimentation on sperm, eggs, embryos; and the selling of babies for greed.

Yes, scripture speaks out on this worldly practice of altering life for profit that is inconsistent with biblical standards. The godly man who is in line with God's will can see the light of his spiritual common sense that will allow him to help others with a clear conscience. If that involves helping someone to have a child or increase their happiness by using and inventing creative tools that are exercised with clear sound intent, then it is at that time that we have the green light! It is permissible to adopt children from other races. Don't let anyone confuse you with his or her unreasonable ideas of adoption.

Myth 29: I am a worthless, no-good sinner and that is all I will ever be. If I sin as a Christian, I am to consider myself as a second-class Christian (see Titus 2:11–15; John 3:16; Romans 1:17; Hebrews 6:13–20, 10:19–25; Galatians 5; 1 John 1:9; Ephesians 2:6–7).

This lie has been circulated among Christians for hundreds of years. Yes, that's correct, it is a falsehood that has deceived many Christians into believing that although we are sinners saved by grace, we are nothing but a bunch of worthless boat anchors that do not have a right to be free and a right to be happy and prosperous. Why is this concept of being worthless and second class a lie attributed to born-again Christians? Are we not really sinners according to Romans 3:23 and that we are worthy of death according to Romans 6:23?

Well, the reason why many Christians feel that they are worthless and not good for anything stems from the teaching and misinterpretation of passages of the scripture that tell us that we are sinners and worthy of death and that all liars are going to hell, and in order to follow Christ, we must deny ourselves daily. Many Christians think that living in poverty and cutting yourself off from the world pleases God, and it is an example to the unbelievers of this world that our God is a good God who demonstrates His love through those who are willing to cast off the sinful desires of the world and condition themselves to live like worthless slaves for God that promises some love, joy, and peace in this life and in the life to come.

The idea of a worthless sinner is grounded in the idea that the Christian who exhibits the lifestyle of a pauper demonstrates to the world that we can believe by this example that our God will provide for our happiness and well-being based on our sacrifices, baloney! This kind of thinking is cruel and in bad taste. There is a time and a place for sacrifice and servanthood. Your head must be in the right place to perform a dedicated or part-time Christian service and being a servant with a happy heart.

God does not want us to live like paupers and throw away our personalities, our wealth, and our material goods or live like a worthless boat anchor. Our calling and obedience is not based on preemptive aims, goals, respect, or a right to life because we have salvation and the unbeliever is lost. Many Christians believe in that line of thought today. Their mind has been polluted with the misinterpretation of servanthood and sacrifices that result in all for God and nothing for me.

Requirements and Expectations

What God does require of the Christian is obedience to His commandments and that we love one another. God wants us to be happy, and yes, we have net worth as Christians. We are not a bunch of worthless sinners that only have a place in this life only to live a shameful and wasteful existence. It is true that man has fallen into sin and that he deserves death. But God has demonstrated His love for us by sending Jesus Christ into this world to redeem a people for Him. We are created in the image of God, and the blood of Christ has redeemed us for all our iniquities. We receive the promises and inheritances that God promises to those who love Him.

Considerations

If we were nothing but a bunch of worthless sinners with no goals and ambitions in life to succeed, how come God chose Mary to bear the child of the Holy Ghost called Jesus? How come Jesus Christ said that we are worth more than many sparrows? Why did Jesus Christ choose the twelve apostles to preach the gospel to all? How come God chose Paul the apostle to be a powerful preacher and made an example to the rulers of this world? The Bible teaches that Jesus Christ is the Son of God and that we are being called out among the sinful ways of this world to serve a Holy God that loves His people and will deliver them from the curse of the evil that is in this world!

Declaration

We are not worthless, and we should not think of ourselves as not good for anything. We have a right to life, and we have the right to God's promises to live a happy life full of joy that comes from serving a loving God that calls us from our sinful state into a glorious state of being.

Myth 30: I lose my earthly rights because I am now born again and have no earthly value because I am a servant of God (see Acts 25, 26; Colossians 2, 3; Titus 2:11–15).

No one loses his or her rights as a Christian. This very destructive myth has sprung up in many Christian circles because their belief is that the scriptures teach us that our citizenship is in heaven and we are not of this world anymore. Parallel to that thought is the additional insulting myth is the attitude that we have salvation; the unbeliever is lost and since we are being called out from among this world, our position of acceptance of this salvation results in the justification and acceptance of our loss of rights here on Earth, baloney!

If you think we don't have rights, talk to the mothers and fathers of the dead and wounded sons and daughters that served in the armed forces that helped to protect and preserve your freedom! Why don't you stop into your local VFW Post and ask to see one of the members that was caught and tortured by the enemy in a POW Camp? Ask a lawyer why he or she serves as a protector of those who have been wronged by unscrupulous criminals who have broken the law and you are the victim?

How about asking the local prosecutor in your town who seeks justice for the families of the victims where a criminal has taken the life of a person for selfish reasons? Perhaps you could visit your local police department and ask the officers why they will put their life on the line to protect your earthly rights? Or how about the case where an accident has taken place and it requires the services of professionals who are competent to testify on your behalf! Think about it!

Wise up, Christian friend, you have rights. The author will stand up and be counted among those who believe that we have earthly rights, value, and dignity as persons. Take a stand for your rights and don't take any nonsense from those who teach something different.

In the book of Acts 25 and 26, Paul the apostle appealed to Caesar for his right to defend himself as a Roman citizen. If you do not know much about that system, the bottom line is that in Paul's day as a Roman citizen, he was considered a free and dignified citizen with all the rights, privileges, and value due him from their concept of a just government. A Roman citizen was considered as the top of the lot. They were first class in everything as a Roman citizen! Put this into your thinking cap. If you do not have rights as a Christian citizen, why register to vote, why enlist in the armed forces, and why do you pay attention to the laws of the land that are instituted by the local governments? Why should you support freedom in America or wherever you live?

Don't let some tricky theologian or misguided Christian con you into believing that you do not have rights as a Christian. We all have rights, value, and dignity that God gave to us when He created us in His image. We have rights, which are authorized through the declarations of the God-ordained institutions on Earth. We are to live as free men and women; we are governed by God's servants with God as the head of all governments. The only thing we give up when we become a born-again Christian is our sin. Think about it.

Myth 31: Christians do not have the right to change their pursuits if they have already dedicated themselves to one type of service for God (see Matthew 6:25–34; Matthew 7:7–8; Galatians 5:1; Colossians 3:17; James 3:17–18).

This idea has been propagated by some Christians who believe that once you make a decision for the type of service to God, you must stay with that decision because this is God's will for your life. An example of this kind of mentality is the case of a person who decides to be a single missionary, and later on in life, he or she feels it is time for a change and get married and raise a family. Opposition to this kind of change is held by many Christians because they believe that you are called for one type of service and that's it. What a myth! If you want to change your mind about the type service you feel qualified for, then do it and ask no questions. You have a free will to make choices and change your vocation as many times as necessary for your growth and peace of mind in your service to God.

Myth 32: Christians should always volunteer their services and expect to either work for nothing or work for very low wages (see Matthew 10:5–10; Colossians 3:17).

Christians have exploited this idea for years. Many Christians are on a guilt trip about the level of wages they get for their services. They think that once you become a Christian, you are to live in poverty for the rest of your life because you should be an example like Jesus. The example was that Jesus had no place to lay his head and denied Himself and took up his cross daily.

Jesus also said the worker is worthy of his wages. You should be paid the fair market value for the type of service you offer. Some people make two hundred dollars a week while others make thousands of dollars a day and more. Each service is different and so is the circumstance that surrounds the job and the organization that offers the job. It is true we should volunteer our services when we can, but to let some organization walk all over us and take advantage of us because we are Christians is just plain nonsense.

Some Christians also promote the idea that you should get things for free or have them donated to you because you are a poor, suffering Christian, baloney! You are to work for your living just like the unbeliever. God will provide for you in many ways, and He will send you gifts that you do expect to come your way. If you exhibit the poor-me attitude, it only represents a shoddy example of what the Christian life is really about. If you want to work for low wages that is your business. If you have a guilt trip about earning large sums of money, keep it to yourself. There are plenty of rich Christians who appreciate what they have, and they are thankful that they are wise stewards of their wealth. Going first class is not wrong!

Myth 33: Unbelievers are not nice people (see Matthew 7; Romans 2).

This lie springs from the conceptual myth that unbelievers are ugly, unfair, dirty, and generally not nice because they have not accepted Christ as their savior. I got news for you, unbelievers have a right to life just as much as Christians. Who are you to judge others? You were an unbeliever before you accepted Christ. So if you knock them, you are knocking yourself.

Jesus said sinners love sinners. We know according to God's word unbelievers are condemned to judgment and will face the wrath of God. God has ordained and decreed that we can only come into His presence through Christ. We know that the unbeliever is condemned to spend eternity in outer darkness if he does not come to Christ. Don't judge others and justify your judgment because you have salvation, and they don't. You should tell them of the love of Christ so they can join us. Let God handle the judging of men's souls.

Myth 34: Christians and unbelievers should not work together (see Matthew 7).

This position is a choice that Christians make and has nothing to do with the interpretation of the scripture. The world is not Christianized, and we must accept the reality that unbelievers are a necessary part of our coexistence. Christians and unbelievers must work together to achieve God's goal of winning the lost to Christ. Some Christians choose to work only in Christian organizations so they avoid working with unbelievers. That is okay if you want to do that but don't knock the people who work in mixed company. There are a lot of us who are called by God to apply and utilize the spiritual tools God has given us to work with unbelievers. It is an opportunity to witness and preach the gospel to the lost.

Myth 35: Christian women don't wear expensive clothes and fine jewelry (see Colossians 2; 1 Peter 3:3–4).

It's not true. If you can afford nice clothes or a luxury item, then you have the right to buy them. We need to apply our wealth in the right places. The message is that we are to buy what is necessary for our survival. However, if you have been blessed with wealth, then it is your free choice to buy what you want.

We do not need the hottest car on the block to go eat your ice cream cone and diamond-studded dresses to impress the world. But we do need to dress in an appropriate manner when we are working in circles that demand better clothes and better material goods. If you can afford something special and you have the wealth, then go and make the purchase and move on with your life. Dump the guilt trip. It is your money, and you are the steward of it.

Please don't get upset about the passage in 1 Peter 3 where the apostle Peter says that women should not wear expensive clothes and fine jewelry. Peter said women should let the inner person shine for Christ and not expensive clothes. Don't complicate your life with expensive material goods that are not in good taste. Our inner person should shine and glorify God, not our material things. We need to keep our minds humble in the perspective of keeping our minds on Christ and not on the material goods.

To further clarify, Peter was talking to a certain type of individual who buys expensive clothes and jewelry just to impress people. Nice clothes make you feel good, but if you are buying them with thoughts of putting someone down, that is a sin.

Myth 36: Christians do not fight in wars (see Ecclesiastes 3; Romans 13).

It is very clear that the scripture teaches that Christians must fight in time of war if they are called to do so by their government. There are many examples of God's people fighting for their rights in the Old Testament. The Hebrews fought many wars against many enemies, and God was at their side and the Hebrews won. In the

New Testament, Romans 13, it says that the government does not bear the sword for nothing. To paraphrase Jesus when He was being persecuted, He said, "Now is not the time for me to wage war if it was so, my angels would be fighting for me."

When you live in a powerful country and your might is right, many nations want to usurp that power. They want to be number 1. It is part of man's conscience to conquer and rule over others. This conquering mindset is magnified from Genesis because God has given us the authority and power to rule over all of the animals and beasts of the world. In any society or culture, there must be an order to it. The scriptures teach that we have the right to appoint leaders to rule over us because they keep watch over us. Some leaders want to usurp their authority and rule over nations with which they have no right to rule over. This is where man distorts his authority given by God in Genesis, to rule over all animals and beasts of the field.

God appoints all rulers of all governments whether they know it or not! Jesus Christ told Pontius Pilate that he (Pilate) had authority given to him from above. God gives authority to man, and when man's evil desires overrule his good conscience, he does evil in the sight of the Lord. Christians do fight in just wars. When you are a soldier in the armed forces, you must do as they tell you within the limits of sound conscience. If going to war is part of your duty, then duty calls. However, you can choose to work in a non-combat job while serving in a combat zone. See it is not complicated. Trust the Lord and your spiritual common sense, and you will fit in.

Myth 37: The love of money is the root of all evil (see 1 Timothy 6:10; 1 Timothy 4:4–5; 1 Timothy 6:3–5).

This passage has been misinterpreted by hundreds of pastors and millions of Christians. Yes, that's right; this misinterpretation of this passage has infiltrated our churches and Christian organizations. The net result of this misinterpretation has sent many Christians into fits of rage, disbelief, and just plain guilt over the ownership, use, and application of money. This misguided interpretation about money has caused many Christians to leave their churches and their well-paying jobs and live with the feeling that God has cursed money, and there is no redemption for this sin. Guess what, this negative and backward interpretation is totally wrong!

This misinterpretation comes from a distorted translation found in the King James Version. The translation reads, "For the love of money is the root of all evil." Actually, this passage has been mistranslated from the Greek manuscripts. The Greek version reads, "For a root of all evils is the love of money." The New American translation reads, "For the love of money is a root of all sorts of evil and some by longing for it have wandered away from the faith and pierced themselves with many a pang." By using your spiritual common sense, you can see that by comparing this passage in the King James Version with the NASV and the Greek text, you will see clearly this passage has been misquoted. The key words are love, root, a, of, all, and money. Think about it.

If you think money is the root of all evil, consider these points:

1. How do you explain the transgression of the sin of Adam and Eve recorded in Genesis?

2. If money was the root of all evil, how do you explain the root of evil in societies and cultures that do not involve money?

3. How do you explain the passage in Romans 3:23 that says, "All have sinned and fall short of the glory of God?"

4. How do you explain Romans 6:23 that says, "For the wages of sin is death, but the free gift of God is eternal life through Jesus Christ our Lord.

5. How do you explain Romans 5:12 that says, "Therefore, just as sin entered the world through one man, and death through sin, and in this way death came to all men, because all sinned."

6. Explain John 3:16: "For God so loved the world that He gave His only begotten Son, that whoever believes in Him should not perish, but have eternal life."

7.   Exegete 1 Peter 4:15–16, "By no means let any of you suffer as a murderer, or thief, or evildoer, or a troublesome meddler; but if anyone suffers as a Christian, let him not feel ashamed, but in that name let him glorify God."

8.   Explain Titus 2:11–14:

> For the grace of God has appeared, bringing salvation to all men, instructing us to deny ungodliness and worldly desires and to live sensibly, righteously and godly in the present age, looking for the blessed hope and the appearing of the glory of our great God and Savior, Christ Jesus; who gave Himself for us, that he might redeem us from every lawless deed and purify for Himself a people for His own possession, zealous for good deeds.

Summation

There are many cultures on planet Earth that do not use money as a means of buying or selling services and goods. When Adam and Eve sinned in the Garden of Eden, money was not present in their world. Sin was introduced by the transgression of Adam and Eve's disobedience to a command from God. Sin entered this world through the act of disobedience of one man and one woman. This is how the presence of evil entered into the heart of man. Man is spiritually dead in his sins and trespasses. He needs the Holy Spirit of God to redeem him from the curse of sin and death.

Money has nothing to do with human's sinful state based on the transgression recorded in Genesis. Then how does money become evil to man? The truth is that man created money, and he is the one who is responsible to be a good steward of it. That means to use money for good. It does not mean that money is generically and inherently evil or man is evil because he has possession of money. Please get it straight.

Money is a wonderful, powerful tool that we have that allows us to buy and sell what we need. Our American culture is based on money to support our capitalistic system. We are responsible for the proper use and application of our money.

In the American culture as well as other civilized cultures, we all need money to pay our rent and our mortgages, buy food, invest in the ministry, and enjoy the fruits of our labor. This passage on money and the love of it mistranslated from the King James Version should serve as warning to all. You as a Christian can be tricked into believing something is wrong and sinful when in reality the use and application of that tool decides its motive. Any tool whether it is money or a spiritual gift can be used to generate good or evil. When you who know in your heart that you can detect an error in this kind of preaching, you should not commit yourself to fatalism and accept it. You must use your spiritual common sense to sort out what is right. Jesus said, "The truth will set you free." The truth that will set us free is the guidance of Holy Spirit who indwells us. He causes our minds to know and understand the truth in Christ Jesus.

Myth 38: Sex is only for procreation and anything else is not permissible, and it is sinful to enjoy any type of sexual activity as a married couple (see Ecclesiastes 9:9; Songs of Solomon).

This sorry teaching has created serious hardships for many Christians. Sex was given to man and woman for procreation and fun. That's right, you narrow-minded, stereotyped theologians. Sex is for fun in the marriage bed only! Do you think God would have given us something so special and so sacred as to have us believe that it is only for procreation? Ask yourself these questions:

1. Why is it that a man and a woman's body are specially designed to fit together for the act of lovemaking?
2. Why do women have a special organs called the clitoris, which is designed just for sexual pleasure?
3. Why do you think a man is capable of producing over two hundred million sperm in seventy-two hours?

4.	Why is it that men and women experience relief from tension when they reach orgasm?

5.	Why do you think God programmed a man and a woman's body to be emotionally and spiritually prepared for lovemaking and to enjoy climaxes?

6.	Why is sex drive the most powerful emotion in men and women?

Sex is a natural function that bonds the physical relationship in marriage. It is a proof of spiritual love consummated in a physical act. Think about it.

Summary

To say that sex is only for procreation is unacceptable. God originally designed the human body with all the accouterments and attributes for work and play. We have a right to enjoy ourselves and to enjoy sex. Stop worrying about what other people think! Do your own thing and enjoy yourself. Keep theology out of your bedroom where it is not in context.

Read the Songs of Solomon, the Psalms and the Proverbs. You will find that men and women loved and enjoyed each other. Yes, sex is a part of marriage but not all of it. Do what you think is best in your own bedroom and stop getting hang-ups on some theologians twisted idea of sex only for procreation. Sex is a special bonding effect on a marriage. Sex is the one act that is intimate, sacred, and personal between a husband and wife. It is the only act where a man and a woman actually share and transmit the life force or energy that flows in the body and soul.

To say that sex is only for procreation is not a biblical truth. The design and the obvious functions of certain organs dictate that humans are sexual beings. There is no scripture to support the twisted idea of sex for procreation only. This act is sacred between a man and a woman. Jesus did not teach sex for procreation. The scriptures do not condemn sex in the institution of marriage. As a matter of fact, the scriptures say let the marriage bed be undefiled. Enjoy, enjoy, and enjoy.

Myth 39: God sits on His throne in heaven and watches everything we do on giant TV screens in order to get feedback to control and adjust mankind's behavioral patterns (see Genesis 1; Psalm 139:7; Ephesians 1:11; John 4:24; Hebrews 4:12–13).

Some Christians believe that in order for God to know where we are, He must have some super-powerful telecommunications system that reaches into our lives and operates unknown to us and in complete secrecy. This idea is so stupid and immature that it makes the author wonder how small the human mind can lower itself to placing God in their spiritual fishbowl of ignorance and stupidity. The power of Almighty God escapes no one.

If you check the scriptures, you will read that God is everywhere. We cannot hide from Him. God is omnipresent, omnipotent, and omniscient. God transcends all things. God's spirit is everywhere throughout the universe. God is not limited to time and space. To paraphrase a statement made by Jesus, He Said, "Where you are I am." Please believe that God does not need our technology to run His creation. God has His own system, and we cannot see it or understand it. We can only accept and trust in what our spirit and our senses reveal to us.

Myth 40: The Sabbath, Sunday, the Lord's Day and the day of the Lord are all the same (see Genesis 2:3; Exodus 20:11, 31:1; Matthew 24:30–51, 25:13; Romans 14:5–6; 2 Peter 10–13).

Many Christians are confused the about Sabbath day, the Lord's Day and the day of the Lord. All of the above are separate and distinct days. Christians need to read their Bibles with diligence and with a spirit of critical judgment. It will open their mind to God's plan for man/women through the ages. These plans are revealed through distinct dispensational time periods.

Consider these points:

1. The Sabbath was a day of rest ordained and commanded by God, which was given to the Old Testament Hebrews. This day was part of the law that the Israelites followed with strict obedience.
2. The Lord's Day is the day in which the Lord Jesus Christ was resurrected from the grave after his crucifixion.
3. The day of the Lord is a day in which Jesus Christ will return to Earth and select out Christians from among the non-Christians. This will be a day of judgment.

Christians have confused the Sabbath day of rest with the idea that Sunday is now equal to the Sabbath and that Sunday now assimilates the Sabbath day. This is wrong and when Christians push the idea that Sunday is the Sabbath, they are making a major misinterpretation of the scripture.

Observations

A. The Sabbath and Sunday are not the same day.
B. When we say that Sunday is the only day for rest, we are forcing Christians to accept and believe a legalistic lie.
C. We should take one day for rest, but it does not have to be Sunday.
D. Church services do not have to be held only on Sunday.
E. We are not under the law but under grace.

Christians are responsible for implementing the legalistic concept that the Lord's Day represents a day of worship. This is in correlation to the resurrection of the Lord Jesus Christ after He was nailed to the cross for our sins.

Through the centuries, Christians have claimed Sunday as the day of rest. However, nowhere in scripture does it say that Christians must worship on Sundays only. The scriptures do not make the

Sabbath and Sunday equal with each other. In fact, the Sabbath was a Saturday.

God implemented a mandate for the Hebrews to worship on the Sabbath because God wanted the Hebrews to set aside a day of worship for Him. God was the head of the government (theocracy) for the nation of Israel, and the Sabbath day helped bring to each man's conscience a reminder to the people of Israel that God Almighty was their God and that they should worship Him in reverence and awe that the God of gods, the Creator of the universe permitted Himself to have a personal relationship with His people. Yes. that's right, God was the Hebrew's government.

The law, which lasted about 430 years, included a Sabbath day. This day allowed the Hebrews to take one day off a week and rest from their daily chores. It did not mean that you went into your house and locked all your doors and spent the next twenty-four hours as a hermit. Although it was very close to that level of thinking, it did have some flexibility. Such necessities of life were permissible on that day. When Jesus walked on this Earth, many of the miracles that He performed were on the Sabbath. The Hebrews were enraged to the point where they plotted to kill Jesus because they had isolated the Sabbath day as a day in which no one was to work or use as a day that contributed to their normal routine.

It's so amazing that the human mind is so corrupt that even when his good sense tells him he is doing wrong, he still plots out evil against his brother. What is so amazing is that the Hebrews actually walked with Jesus Christ, the Creator of the universe, and they wanted to kill him because they thought that keeping the Sabbath justified the precedence over every other form of thought. How can man be so blind? There is always a way out or some flexibility built into any system that is not an absolute. The Sabbath was not an absolute; it was a Commandment of the Law of Moses.

We are bound by God's absolutes, and we are responsible and held accountable to obey God's Commandments. We are to obey the commandments and follow the guidelines that the scriptures give us. However, we are not to create a legalistic approach to something that for all practical considerations has flexibility built into it.

One of the commandments says, "Thou shall not murder." This commandment means you shall not kill (murder) for the sake of destroying one another for personal gain. However, it is permissible to kill in time of war or self-defense or kill animals for food. Please be careful when reading absolutes and commandments. We are to enjoy our lives, and not make fools of ourselves with boat anchors tied around our necks because we believe in a system that binds us to seek the truth and causes us to sacrifice our common sense just so we can please God. Remember Jesus said, "The truth will set you free."

Myth 41: Working on Sunday is a sin (see Romans 14:5–8; Romans 14:23; Colossians 3:17; Titus 2:13–14).

This thinking is a tripwire in a minefield of bombs, negative programming, and gross misinterpretation of the scripture. These mindsets and attitudes originate from Christians who believe we should not work on Sundays because God will condemn us if we do. In another words, Sunday is sacred, and it should be reserved as a Sabbath or non-workday and official day where the world stops to take a breath and gets its bearings. Give me a break. Did you ever hear of such stupidity? Where in the world do Christians get the idea that Sunday is limited to some sort of officially ordained day as a non-workday?

The next time you need immediate medical-emergency care, ask the hospital if they have shut down because it is Sunday? Why don't you tell all the pregnant mothers in town that doctors don't deliver babies at 2:00 a.m. on Sunday? Why don't you ask the police department to knock off on Sunday because the criminals are taking a break? Tell the water company, electric company, and all vital services that Sunday is a rest period. Please don't get legalistic about Sunday. We live in a complex and sophisticated society where many of us work on Sunday and take a break on a different day. As a matter of fact, many pastors take Mondays off. Think about it. Jesus said, "The truth will set you free."

Myth 42: Because I am a Christian, it is wrong to learn of myself, discover myself, believe in myself, develop myself, and enjoy myself (see Proverbs 29:18; Ecclesiastes 9:7; Galatians 5:16' Ephesians 2:6–7; Ephesians 3:14–19; Colossians 3:15–17; Colossians 2 and 3; 1 Timothy 4:4).

In many Christian circles, we are taught that it is wrong or sinful to discover ourselves. This mentality suggests that you should throw your life away and forget your own wants and needs so you can be a vessel fit for God's use. Without a shadow of doubt, this twisted idea is a distortion of the scripture. What did you say? Just as sure as God made the sun, I know for a fact this trick is being taught in many Christian organizations. It is nothing short of brain corruption and negative programming. It comes from those who believe that you cannot be a worthy servant of God if you desire to use your free will.

If any Christian teaches this kind of thinking, he or she needs help. Where in the Bible does it say that we have to give up our lives and throw it away and give up our individuality to become a better servant? Contrary to this teaching, the scriptures are clear that you must expand your horizons as you grow and mature in God's grace. "Without a vision, the people will perish." Go look it up. (Proverbs 29:18)

To paraphrase a statement made by our Lord Jesus Christ, "He who loses his life for my sake will find it." What does this statement mean? In order to find your real self, you need to turn your life over to Christ. You need to let God put your life in order by allowing Christ on the throne of your life. Turning your life over to Christ does not throw away your treasures. Instead, you are by faith giving yourself over to God to manage and bless your life. That was the exact message Jesus was teaching his disciples. Come follow me. These treasures consist of talents, gifts, services, and materials goods to be supervised, managed, and increased by the Lord Jesus Christ in the power of the Holy Spirit. Amen.

Clarification

You need to pray to God to help you find yourself. Develop your talents and gifts for God's service and through that process, you will learn of the riches of Christ. As you cultivate and develop your talents and gifts, you can transfer some of those energies to personal time for your own pleasure. During your lifetime, you need to implement time for your own self-satisfaction. In other words, you need time off. You need time away from your job. You need a toy in your life. As a matter of fact, you have a right to have many toys. All work and no play are totally out of place.

Conclusion

The scriptures teach that in six days, God made the heavens and the earth. On the seventh day, He rested from His work. You rest from your work and discover the things you like to do. We must have balance in our lives, and toys are part of that balance. What toys? Find something for yourself that you can enjoy, boating, golf, tennis, bowling, cars, computers, sewing, clubs, photography, flying, and whatever. Just find a toy for yourself. Don't feel guilty about enjoying your life. If your toy takes you away from your main goal, then you are not assigning your priorities correctly. Remember balance is the key. Look at the examples of Jesus. He took time off from His work. Just read the gospels, and you will see it.

Read Ecclesiastes 3. Balance is the key to being a faithful servant. You are doing the will of God, and you will be at peace with God. Many Bible scholars believe that God created the heavens and the earth in six literal twenty-four-hour earth days. What do we really know about it? Is it that important? There are many guesses at it, but you know the passage. One day is like a thousand years, and a thousand years is like one day. Don't get caught up in a conversation that goes in circles. What do we care if God created the heavens in six days or six million years? It changes nothing in your little life that is like a vapor. A balanced Christian life is a continual building-block concept that will help you to be the best in Christ Jesus.

Myth 43: It is wrong to take a Christian to court (see Matthew 5:21–26; Colossians 3; 1 Timothy 4:4).

This error has been chasing Christians around in circles for many years. When a Christian is applying the principles of the scripture, he or she must be able to make the adjustments between what the Bible says on Christian conduct and what his culture or his society demands under law and constitution. Christians are bound by two systems of authority.

1. A Christian is a citizen of heaven.
2. A Christian must obey God's laws.
3. A Christian must obey the local laws.

When the Bible speaks of taking Christians to court, it means that you should try to stay out of court on trivial matters. Let the trivial business be judged by your peers or the church. However, if you are involved in anything beyond a trivial matter, then you will most likely have to spend time in a courtroom. Please don't be misled by those who believe in the absolute of not taking Christians to court. It is not true, and it will not work in our culture.

God ordains the court system. Even if the magistrates are unbelievers, you still have the right and the obligation to settle your disputes in a godly manner. Don't take the law into your own hands and commit sin, which is greater than the problem you are dealing with. Use your spiritual common sense.

Myth 44: Christians can be possessed by demons (see Ecclesiastes 12:6–7; Romans 12:21; Acts 10:36; Ephesians 4:30; John 10:27–28; John 3:16; 1 John 4:4).

This lie is straight out of hell! Some Christians believe that while you are a true born-again believer, you can be possessed by a demon if you commit sin and turn away from God. The scriptures are clear that there is no way that a child of God a true believer can be possessed by a demon. Just as sure as God made the heavens and the earth a born-again Christian is safe from demon possession. However, any Christian can be influenced by a demon. The scriptures warn us that the devil sets up snares and traps and is like a roaring lion seeking whom he may devour. Be aware that the power of Satan is very strong. He can appear in many forms. The devil and his fallen spiritual comrades are committed to do nothing but destroy human beings and frustrate God's plan. Don't ever underestimate the power and trickery of Satan and demons. You can be tricked into believing that you are possessed, and demons are controlling your life. Satan lives in the spiritual world, and we are not permitted by God to live in that world in the flesh. It is a dimension that we cannot fully understand because we are limited to our physical senses.

Many books have been written about demon possession, and some have even indicated that Christians who are saved were also under demonic possession. The author's advice in this spiritual warfare is to stay away from any kind of demonic game or test with spirits that you do not understand. Some people who have been in Satanic churches or have even been in the little-known cult called the brotherhood have lived and served Satan at the highest levels. They saw demons and Satan. Some women have even been brides of Satan. The men are warlocks. When these people came to Christ, they had to close the doors to Satanic influence. It may take hours, days, or weeks to clear your open pathways to close out the attacks from demonic forces. But they will be closed.

Although you are saved and washed in the blood of Christ, powerful evil forces are still trying to draw you back and want total control. Only Jesus Christ can save you and close those doors. You cannot be inhabited by a demon while you are saved. You can be attacked and tricked to the point where you believe you are possessed and not cleansed. Satan and his evil angels have great power of deception and can use spiritual influence to trick you and cause you fall even to the point of worshipping demonic things. The masons, Mormons Jehovah's Witnesses, and Catholic Church are clear examples of this power, especially the Catholic Church, is considered in many evangelical circles as the great whore in the book of revelation.

Homosexuality, lesbianism, drug addiction, and living and traveling in the gay circles are examples of demon attraction and power of influence.

There are pathways from this physical world to the spiritual world. We can astral project to these places and see through spiritual windows or even be in the spirit world. Be careful. Don't play with your life. If you break the silver cord, you are dead to the physical world and will be transported to the spiritual one. Only God knows what will happen to you.

Conclusion

As born-again believers, our souls are sealed by the Holy Spirit, and we are secure from any possession of the devil. Please remember that the devil is a super-powerful, totally evil spirit. It can send evil thoughts to your mind and play spiritual trickery on you at the highest levels of consciousness that will confuse you and make you believe in lies and false light. The devil deals on the same thought frequency as your thought frequency. The devil knows that when it sends these messages, any person can fall into its trap. The devil cannot read your mind, but it knows when it is playing your number. Christians can detect the devil very easily by recognizing that anything that is against good, clear, sound judgment is of the devil. Jesus said, "Resist the devil, and he will flee from you."

Please don't believe any person that says a Christian can be demon possessed. It cannot happen. Think about it, if a Christian could be possessed by a demon, then where is our eternal security going to come from? Greater is He that is in us than he is in the world. If God cannot save us from the devil, then who can? Please accept that Jesus Christ is God and that He has all the power and all the authority. The Bible is clear that Jesus Christ is Lord and Savior. Believe it! Read the gospels, and you will see it for yourself.

Myth 45: Culture should not be considered when witnessing for Christ (see Matthew 28:18–20, 9:37–38; Colossians 3:17; Revelation 22:18–19).

In America, people think like Americans. In Africa, people think like Africans. In Asia, people think like Asians. It all boils down to the reality that no matter what country you come from, you have a particular inculcation of mindsets and attitudes that are unique to your culture. Your modus operandi is partially molded from the influence of the general sphere of how your particular culture or society accepts certain behavioral patterns for normal daily living. Each culture or society has unwritten rules that reflect the mindsets of values that are unique to that culture.

Example of varying mindsets is in America, it is acceptable for women to wear short dresses. In Africa, bare breasts are acceptable in public. In remote villages, the locals wear no clothes. In America, we are free to choose a marriage partner, the type of job we have, and engage in free enterprise. In contrast to some countries, the government decides the type of job you will have, your parents arrange your marriage, and there is no free enterprise.

What has this to do with witnessing for Christ? Effective witnessing for Christ in cultures and societies that are different from your own requires that you to learn of their ways. In the New Testament, Paul put himself in other people's shoes or situation in order to reach them for Christ. We do not accept all the ways of other cultures in order to reach them for Christ. But we have to respect other people's cultures and way of life to witness to them on their level.

If you look at the original language of the New Testament, you will discover that it was written in Koine. That level of Greek was the common language of the people of that culture in that time period. If the New Testament were written for the first time today, it would probably be inspired in English. When we share the gospel to other cultures, we must take into account their habits and language patterns. Some words that we use in our language library do not agree with words in other cultures' libraries.

Here is test question. How do you explain the parable of talents to a culture that does not have or use money? That is a tough question. How do you handle it? Why not approach it with spiritual common sense. Why not rewrite the passage to conform to that cultures' language differences? Think about it!

In many cases, Bible translators must rewrite or rephrase certain passages in the Bible to conform to the language patterns of various cultures. Please don't get the idea that we are going to be condemned by God because we are rewriting the language or the words of the scripture. Bible translators are only refocusing the text of the scripture to conform to the context of the message of the scriptures so other cultures can believe and understand the message of salvation in Christ Jesus. Think it over.

Myth 46: It is wrong for a Christian to lie (see Revelation 21:8; Colossians 3:17; 1 Timothy 4:1).

This is the big one, the big kahuna. It is a delicate subject because as a Christian, we are to trust God that He will deliver us from all evil, and through the power of the Holy Spirit, we will live a victorious Christian life. We are to speak the truth, be on good terms with all men, and slander no one. This is all fine in the ideal world of Christian living. However, because we live in a world that is sliding itself downhill to hell as fast as it can, the world clearly demonstrates its direct opposition to God's systems of living by faith. To be specific, situational ethics enters the picture. A Christian may find himself in a life-and-death struggle with the enemy that in order to preserve life, he must resort to telling a lie to protect a life. Why then should we discuss the issue of a Christian telling a lie? Please read and follow this true story.

On January 23, 1968, an American Navy ship *USS Pueblo* strayed into the Sea of Japan and was captured by the North Koreans. Through the long hours and eleven months of interrogation, torture, and intensive abuse, the crew and the captain were exhausted. During that time of capture, the captain was asked the nature of his business by the enemy. What was his orders concerning his entrance into restricted waters? Well, if the captain told the truth about his spying, which amounted to a secret intelligence–gathering mission, the North Korean Communists could have killed them justifiably for trespassing into its territorial waters.

The captain of the ship was thrust into a situation where in order to protect the lives of his crew, he lied to save his life and his crew. That was a case where situational ethics entered the arena of life and death. The captain had to make a high-level, urgent, top-priority decision that involved the fate of himself and his crew.

Should the captain have told his communist captors the truth of his mission and get himself and his crew imprisoned and or killed for nothing, or should he have told a lie to get himself and the crew off the hook and come home safe and sound to their families? Should he have sacrificed the eighty-one innocent lives and himself because it is better to tell the truth than to tell a lie? Think it over.

This case is true. The man was Capt. Lloyd M. Bucher of the *USS Pueblo*. This situation came to be known as the Pueblo Incident. Consider this point, the captain and his crew were freed only after US officials signed a document apologizing for the alleged spying and promising that no such incident would reoccur. Whether the captain was a Christian or not, the game is the same. Life and death played out on words. How would you have played it?

Clarification

We do not have a license to sin. We are not to abuse our eternal security and our continued forgiveness of sin by lying to one another. We are warned in the scripture not to lie or hurt one another. However, in a situation where a life is in jeopardy and that life hangs in the balance because of what you say, then you must make a high-level decision that involves ethics, which transcends the telling of a lie to save a life. Do you tell the truth for the sake of telling the truth and that is the Christian thing to do? Do you tell the truth to impress your enemy with your conceited knowledge that lying is wrong and telling the truth is always preferred to telling a lie, or do you wake up to the reality that a gun is pointed at your head and by telling a lie to your enemy will save your own neck?

Remember, you owe the enemy nothing, except to tell him that he is lost and needs Jesus Christ as his Savior. There is a time to tell someone about the saving grace of our Lord, and there is a time to keep your mouth shut. In the norm of Christian living, telling lies is sin and in opposition to the norm of telling the truth. But in a situation where telling the truth to your enemy will get you killed, then you must make a sensible, moral, high-level decision to save your own life. It's up to you.

Myth 47: Christians and Purgatory (see Luke 23:32–43).

This is one of the biggest and most destructive lies ever to come out of a church official's mouth. Some Christian's believe that there is a second chance to be redeemed from sin in this life once they have passed through the corridor of death. In addition, some Christians believe that all your sins are not forgiven or accounted for by God in this life and so you must work off those sins in a spiritual place called purgatory. If you believe in this thinking, you do not understand eternal security that is in John 10:27–28, John 3:16, Hebrews 9:27–28, Hebrews 10:15–18, Titus 2:13–14, and Romans 10:9–10.

What is the main point of these passages?

1. We have eternal security in Christ Jesus.
2. God sent His only Son into the world so that through Him we would be saved.
3. Jesus Christ is the sufficient sacrifice for all sins, and we will face him for judgment at the end of this life, not for sin, but for deeds done in the body.
4. Jesus Christ is God and Savior who redeemed us from all our sins.

We have salvation in Christ, and all our sins are forgiven. When this life is over, we will be judged in righteousness and not sin, and we will be assigned a place in God's heavenly kingdom. The idea of purgatory has been introduced by the Roman Catholic Church as a cover up for their misunderstanding and unbelief of salvation by faith through God's grace. It is also a misunderstanding of the word Hades, which means hell.

Some Christians believe that when you die and go to heaven, you actually go to a waiting place, which is a facsimile of heaven because according to the New Testament, God has not passed judgment on the earth and has not ushered in the new kingdom that is discussed in the book of Revelation. The truth is that there is a waiting place in heaven called paradise. We do know that the promise made from the past about the Savior belongs to those in the Old Testament. When the thief on the cross said to Jesus, "Remember me when you come into your kingdom." Jesus said, "Truly this day you will be in paradise with me." The thief got saved, and by the way, he did not partake of water baptism. Jesus also said in the scripture, "He that is the least in the kingdom of heaven is greater than anyone on earth" (Matthew 11:11).

Think about this point, if purgatory really existed, why would the New Testament say that Jesus Christ sat down at the right hand of the God the Father after He had made purification for the sins of His people? Read the book of Hebrews; it discusses in detail the ministry of salvation that Jesus Christ provided for mankind. Anyone who teaches purgatory is a liar and is leading those who are unsaved straight to hell. Read Titus 2:11–15 and Revelation 22:12–17.

Myth 48: If I commit sin while I am a Christian, I must tell my friends all about it and give them a detailed outline of the sin, and this is to be done even though I have asked God to forgive me (see 1 John 1:9; Matthew 6:5–14).

This mythical fable of forgiveness has been used against Christians to force them to tell their friends and the church body about their sins. It is believed that it clears your conscience and purifies the body of Christ, baloney! When you accept Christ as your

Savior, your sins are forgiven forever—past, present, and future. If you commit sin as a Christian, you must seek God to cleanse you from your unrighteous act in private.

If your sin involves the abuse of another person, then you need to seek that person out and ask him/her for your forgiveness. This act clears your conscience of your guilt, not your sin. If you have abused a number of people, then you owe them an apology. However, you do not have to blab it to the world, and you don't have to tell other Christians or your friends who are not involved with your problem. Don't get into this self-flagellating mentality where you think that others will respond favorably to your mistakes. Keep a lid on it as much as possible.

Use your spiritual common sense when you are seeking to tell others about your sins. Remember we are saved and washed in the blood of Jesus Christ. Our sins are forgiven and while we are walking in this life through the power of the Holy Spirit, we have an advocate who is the Father. Jesus Christ our Lord forgives us our sins no matter what they are during our growing process in our Christian life.

Please don't be tricked by a misguided Christian who has a counter-productive, peanut-sized view of forgiveness. Your sins are between you and God. If you have offended someone, then go and do what the Bible says for you to do. Make peace with them by telling them you are sorry and ask for their forgiveness. It will clear your mind of guilt, and it will reestablish your friendly communication. Do this if you can by all human means. If you can't rectify your communication with that person, then pray for that person and trust God to vindicate you.

Myth 49: Women are not allowed to speak in church (see 1 Corinthians 14:34–35; Titus 2:1–5).

This is a tough problem for many Christian families today. In most conservative, straitlaced Christian communities, there is the belief that women should stay at home and perform the wife/mother's duties that have been assigned to her, and that is it. In other words, it is a biased view of women being second-class Christian citizens. This mentality is simply bad news. It is generic of counter-productive Christians who advocate preconceived, selfishly selected roles for the wife or the single woman. This selected role says that women must not participate in church services and must keep quiet when attending church. By observation, this is what the passage seems to be saying. So what is the truth here?

In Corinthians 14:34, Paul says, "Women should remain silent in the churches. They are not allowed to speak, but must be in submission, as the law says." Paul is referring to the Jewish Law that was kept by the nation of Israel. Today certain sects of the Jewish religion still separate the women and men from each other during services in the synagogues. How do we relate to this passage in our time and day? We should treat this as a local passage only in which that it was intended for the culture of that day in Corinth.

First of all, women can speak in church. They can hold positions in church as officers as well as lay persons. As for the pastors, the scriptures are clear to me that the office of pastor/teacher is only given to men. It does not mean that women cannot be active in church or allowed to teach. It simply means that God has called men to be pastor/teachers, and women to be support mechanisms to the church. Women are different than men in mind, body, and spiritual gifts.

Today in America, we have women pastors. I see no mention in the scripture if it is agreeable or not. I do see a pattern that men were given that gift. Does that mean because men were the head of the household and men were the leaders they got the gift and women were excluded? I don't know. You have to make your own conclusions. I would rather see that women be given the gift of evangelism rather than the gift of pastor/teacher.

The Bible is clear that God gives different gifts to men and women so that they may minister to one another in the body of Christ. When you examine the various gifts that are described in the scripture, keep in mind the order of the creation of man, and you will see that God has appointed man to be the head of the family where the woman is to be the helpmate. It does not make the woman less or second class.

It just makes sense that in God's design of the family system, one person has got to be the leader. Someone has to be first. God placed the male species before the female. It is true in humans, and it is true in the animal world. The male is dominant, and he is the leader. In human relationships, the male is responsible to be the provider, leader, and lover.

In all organized systems or organizations whether it is the family or a business, there is a chain of command that has an order to it. The man's position as a pastor in church is simply at the top of the human chain of authority in the church. Women have a different role in life and a separate role in the church. The woman is to help the man. If you verify the story in Genesis, it is clear that woman was created out of man to be a helpmeet for him.

If you look at the historical perspective in the time period in which the passage about women not speaking in church was written, you would know that in that time period, many women were not as educated as the men, and they were treated as second-class citizens and property of men and or husbands. Does that mean that the Bible is in contempt with today's standards? No, America is a country of equality, and women have a right to teach and speak in the church as well as the home and workplace. This passage about women speaking in church relates to the culture and environment of that particular time period.

Remember the Bible contains local, absolute, timeless, and universal passages. This particular passage was a local passage written in the context of the first-century church with the mindset of Greek/Hebrew culture. Read 2 Corinthians 3:17.

Myth 50: Christians never have personality clashes (see Acts 15:36–41; Ephesians 2 and 3).

This myth is a joke. Many Christians believe that you will always get along with all Christians based on that fact that you have salvation as a common bond, which guarantees instant communication and ratification of any difference of opinion or ego trip, baloney!

The major reason why Christians run into personality clashes and misunderstandings between themselves is very simple. It is based on non-acceptance and belief in the differences of a person's personality, maturity, and spirituality levels, which are some of the themes in this book.

We Christians are blessed with talents, gifts, ideals, ideas, personalities, maturity levels, spirituality, aims, and goals. These attributes combined in our total person are a clear demonstration that God has made each one of us unique. When we ignore these differences in our characters, we ignore the individuality of the person. Some Christians seem to forget that we will have differences of opinion. It is an acceptable part of human nature to have opinions that are different in prospective as it pertains to individuality.

Consideration

Read Acts 15:36–41. These passages discuss a difference of opinion between godly men who were working as apostles, missionaries, and ministers of God. In their process of decision to spread the gospel and further their work for the Lord, they had a disagreement on how they should accomplish the task. They disagreed and discussed the matter then they settled it. If you don't believe that Christians have aims, goals, gifts, personalities, maturity levels, awareness, and spirituality, then you are kidding yourself.

God created man in His own likeness and we as created creatures have a right to life, and we have a character that is unique in its multi-factored human fabric that is woven in likeness from the attributes of God. These attributes are a demonstration of the creativity and longevity of God's love displayed in the human arena of life. These God-like attributes that originate from God are welded into our being, like the twisted pairs of a DNA model.

Please don't sell yourself short because someone is trying to sell you a bill of goods that teaches us that Christians are just empty shells or empty vases ready to do God's will with nothing to start with, as in zero foundation. We are not weaklings, boat anchors, and empty shells that have no right to life or cannot think for ourselves. We are different, and we are unique. We all share a special spiritual bond with Christ Jesus. We are people created in the image of God, and we are to share and help one another live in a system that has been designed as a dependent order of life relying on God for all things. Jesus said, "As much as possible, be on good terms with all men." The author's position is that we should accept ourselves as we are and improve on our total person by being the best in Christ Jesus.

Summation

These fifty myths are a composite picture of varying mind-sets and attitudes that I discovered in my years of travel in America, Russia, and Estonia. Why are Christians hurting one another? Why are Christians lying to one another? Why are Christians their own worst enemy? Why? Because many of us Christians try too hard to get it right.

It is a fact many Christians who believe in and practice the principles in the Word of God also inject legalism and spiritualism into a sound thing. Some Christians are so eager to tell others how wonderful the Christian life is and through that process, introduce the new believer into personal views, legalism, and spiritualism into sound biblical principles.

Proclamation

We have the scriptures, the power of the Holy Spirit, Christian leaders, and our own God-given spiritual common sense. Why are some Christians trying to reinvent the Christian wheel of faith, belief, and practice? My thought is that we need to take a fresh new approach on our Christian living. We need to understand how to live for Christ. We need to exercise the great commandment that Jesus gave us from the beginning, "Love one another as I have loved you."

Consideration

We need to evaluate the shortcomings of our thinking. We are guilty of looking at the little things in a Christian's life and making a major case out of them. Meanwhile, the world is sliding itself down-hill to hell as fast as it can! Why stand by and make a big thing over something that is insignificant? Why attack our Christian brothers and sisters over nonsensical issues? It only causes us to waste valuable time and energy and take away the good works we could be doing in its place. Why create unnecessary havoc and foolish nonsense at the same time and space that it takes to create something good?

We should be devoting our valuable time to building up our brothers and sisters in Christ. We should be respecting and accepting the individuality of each person. Why force others to be rubber stamps of your beliefs and practices that are wasteful and nonproductive? My position is that we see the world through the looking glass, which is our preemptive view of what is Christian and what is non-Christian. It is through this narrow window of theology of values and beliefs that we make judgments based on our interpretation of situations.

All earthly judgments that we make are not to be considered wrong or sinful. When our judgments are hurting one another and causing unnecessary grief to others, it is time to evaluate what is our Christian position. Sin causes pain and suffering. Forgiveness grants settlement through grace.

Why harass Christians for drinking wine, going to the movies, and other insignificant choices? The worldly things that are contrary to God's ways are self-explanatory. These things are what we should be preaching against—adultery, abortion on demand, homosexuality, polygamy, TV programs that degrade women and men, stealing, lying for profit, murder, marriages for convenience, and all sorts of evil that are manifestations of principles that are diametrically opposed to sound biblical teaching.

We need to accept how our culture, personality, maturity levels, spirituality, and values all work in unison to create and form mindsets and attitudes that become either a reality or myth. We need to evaluate and adjust our course of the self that is projecting the manifestation of our beliefs and practices. This manifestation presents our unified character of outward and inward image of beliefs. This projection is based on the principles of the scripture that express an example of a people who are followers of Christ.

Clarification

This is a wake-up call for all Christians. The complex diversity of views, doctrines, beliefs, practices, and rules are so different between the denominations that they cannot be mixed and combined into one central Christian community melting pot. To help alleviate and clear up these unique differences, we who are true Bible-believing, God-fearing, spirit-led people of God should remain in the truth of the scripture. This truth is sufficient without adding our own personal views that are in conflict with the real message of the scriptures.

We as individuals have the right to interpret the scripture and apply its truth to our lives. If we legislate morality codes loosely based on a passage that can be contested on its content, then these loose interpretations can cause unnecessary grief among our brethren. The net result of unnecessary guilt is the self-defeating proposition that takes us away from reaching and accomplishing the goal of living a victorious Christian life.

Conclusion

We Christians must accept and deal with our weaknesses and strengths. The gospel must be preached to all nations. We who preach the gospel of Christ who are responsible for follow-up training must adhere to the full counsel of God. We should not allow our own personal views to override the basic principles and absolutes of the scripture.

We must appeal to the conscience of the lost man. Tell him/her they need Christ as their Savior. The cults are stealing unbelievers and sidetracking believers in great numbers. Why? Because evil and the instant gratification mentality appeals to the mind and human needs, the here and now. Christians do not need the label destroyers of the mind. The cults already have that corner of sin. Let us go forth with the truth that Jesus Christ is Lord and Savior. Christ is our spiritual truth that sets us free. Let us win the lost to Christ and make disciples of them according to the command of Christ Jesus, "Love one another as I have loved you."

PS: After you have read this book and you are still questioning how to get saved by faith, here is the answer, read Romans 10:8–10.

But what does it say? "The word is near you, in your mouth and in your heart." That is, the word of faith, which we are preaching, and if you confess with your mouth to Jesus as Lord and believe in your heart that God raised Him from the dead, you will be saved.

For with the heart, a person believes, resulting in righteousness, and with the mouth, he confesses, resulting in salvation (see http://www.biblegateway.com/passage/?search=Romans%20 10&version=49).

Basically, all you need to do is verbally say, "Dear, Lord Jesus, I am a sinner, and I believe you died for me, and God raised you from the dead. I accept you as my personal Lord and Savior."

That is it! The Holy Spirit will save you and you now will be forgiven and placed spiritually into the body of Christ forever.

ABOUT THE AUTHOR

 Dr. Morris's eclectic background includes business college, comprehensive computer training in programming, operations/system analysis. He also was a computer consultant to major multinational corporations for seven years. He graduated from Northeastern Bible College in Essex Fells, New Jersey, and International Seminary in Plymouth, Florida, in 1984. His ministerial skills include public speaking, counseling, writing, and missions. He served in the US Army's 25th Division in Vietnam and was involved with Artillery Intelligence and was promoted to captain's driver. Dr. Morris is a member of the American Society for Technical Writers. He is also a devoted member to his hometown VFW, American Legion, and the DAV.

His medical training has been provided by the Mountainside Hospital School of Nursing in 1992. Dr. Morris Ministry includes America, Russia, and Estonia. He also has held a number of positions in New Jersey State Government including the Department of State.